ETHNIC CHRONOLOGY SERIES
NUMBER 8

The Germans in America
1607-1970
A Chronology & Fact Book

Compiled and edited by

Howard B. Furer

1973
OCEANA PUBLICATIONS, INC.
DOBBS FERRY, NEW YORK

Library of Congress Cataloging in Publication Data

Furer, Howard B   1934-
    The Germans in America, 1607-1970.

    (Ethnic chronology series, no. 8)
    SUMMARY: The life and contributions of Germans
in America are presented through a chronology and
pertinent documents.
    Bibliography: p.
    1. Germans in the United States--History.
[1. Germans in the United States] I. Title
II. Series.
E184.G3F88   917.3'06'31   72-10087
ISBN 0-379-00506-9

Manufactured in the United States of America

TABLE OF CONTENTS

EDITOR'S FOREWORD

This volume is designed to illuminate a somewhat hitherto-neglected area of America's cultural diversity; namely German immigration to and in the United States. The book includes narrative, analysis and some interpretation of the German experience in America, which has been both important and varied. The Germans have been a special source of interest in ethnic group studies, because, in spite of the rigors and difficulties of the process, they have successfully blended into the American mainstream. This work, in a sense, is an assessment of their contribution to American life.

Despite the fact that many famous German-Americans will be mentioned, this work is not a who's-who of the German element in the United States. Moreover, those Germans who made the greatest sacrifices will remain unknown to the rest of mankind, for the Germans have been part of American history for such a long time, and in such large numbers that individual contributions become relatively unimportant next to the general contributions of the entire group.

What this volume attempts to do, is to examine the social, economic, political, religious, military and cultural experiences of the German people who came to and settled in this country, for their experience is at once complex and valuable. In a short volume of this sort, it is impossible to include all of the facets of the German immigration movement; however, most of the aspects of the German experience have been detailed in highlight form. The chronology section, as well as the documents and bibliography sections will act as excellent starting points for those interested in furthering their knowledge of this subject. Finally, by providing a short, sound, readable book on the life and culture of the German-Americans, it is hoped that this work will produce a good effect, one which all ethnic groups in America seem to need most in our own complex age; understanding and tolerance.

Because the very nature of preparing a chronology of this type precludes the author from using the standard form of historical footnoting, I should like to acknowledge, in the editor's foreword, the major sources used to compile the bulk of the chronological and factual materials comprising the chronology section of this work. They are as follows: Carl Wittke, We Who Built America: The Saga of the Immigrant; Ralph Wood, ed., The Pennsylvania Germans; A. E. Zucker, ed., The Forty Eighters; Richard O' Connor, The German-Americans: An Informal History; and Maldwyn A. Jones, American Immigration.

Howard B. Furer
Newark State College
Union, New Jersey.

CHRONOLOGY

EARLY GERMAN SETTLEMENT – 1607-1800

1607

April 26

Although large groups of Germans would emigrate to America later in the seventeenth century, as early as 1607, three Germans, F. Unger, H. Keffer, and F. Volday were among the hapless followers of Captain John Smith who settled the colony of Jamestown, Virginia. Smith characterized the Germans in the colony as "damned Dutch."

1626

May 4

The first German of prominence in the New World was a Rhinelander named Peter Minuit (Minnewit in German), who was engaged by the Dutch government as director of their colony of New Netherland.

1639

German masons and stoneworkers were brought into the Massachusetts Bay Colony to build up and beautify the prosperous town of Boston.

1663

May

A German Mennonite colony of forty-one was established on the Horekill where it empties into the Delaware. It was a communal settlement, and this Mennonite colony had the first prohibition of slavery on the American continent.

1682

William Penn traveled throughout Germany, and extended an invitation to all those members of persecuted religious sects who wished to leave the old country and come to his colony of Pennsylvania, where they could worship as they pleased.

1683

October 6

A group of Mennonites from the Rhineland, led by a learned Frankfort lawyer, Francis Daniel Pastorius, founded Ger-

1

mantown, Pennsylvania. They had come over on the ship Concord.

November

William Rittenhouse, one of the Mennonite group, built a papermill in Germantown, the first of its kind constructed in America.

The Mennonites started German education in America by founding schools at Germantown and on the Skippack.

1684

A group of Labadists from the Rhineland established a Christian-Communist settlement on the Bohemian River in Maryland. Christian Communism did not thrive in America and the colony broke up in a few years time. Its leader Peter Sluyter, became a wealthy tobacco planter and slave trader.

1688

The earliest protest against Negro slavery in American history was that of the Germantown settlers, whose leader Francis Daniel Pastorius drew up the document. In addition, the German Salzburgers of Georgia, the Germans of the Valley of Virginia, and the Moravians of North Carolina resisted the keeping of Negro slaves as long as was possible.

1690

May

Jacob Leisler, a prominent merchant who had been born at Frankfort-on-Main, was elected the first peoples' governor of New York, and called the first Congress of American colonies. He suffered martyrdom for his independence and public spirit when overcome in 1691 by his enemies.

1701

The German Mennonite settlement at Germantown held its first annual Jahrmarket or annual fair, where the farmers of the surrounding area brought their products for sale.

1707

The first German immigrants arrived in New Jersey, settling in the southern portions of that colony.

1709

The British government shipped Palatine Germans, who had come to England in 1708 in flight from their stricken regions in Germany, to its colony in New York to produce supplies for the Royal Navy, and to guard the frontier against the French.

1710

By 1710, more than 3,000 Palatines settled in the Hudson Valley of New York. Most of them came to America not primarily for religious reasons, but because of economic pressure, which predisposed them to seek wider opportunities. The great majority of Germans were either Lutheran or members of the German Reformed Church, and were called "Church people" to distinguish them from the sectarian sects.

Many Palatine Germans in New York did not like the treatment they received in the Hudson Valley. In addition, they were unhappy with economic conditions there, and several hundred of them migrated, under the leadership of Conrad Weiser, to the Schoharie Valley of New York.

1710

Another large group of Palatines (650 people), led by Baron Christopher de Graffenreid, settled at New Bern, North Carolina.

1711

By 1711, seven Palatine villages had been established in New York on the Robert Livingston manor, and the British government had spent over 100,000 pounds on the settlement project.

1712

The Palatine settlement at New Bern, North Carolina was attacked and nearly destroyed by Indians in the Tuscarora War. As a result, some of the German settlers scattered throughout southeastern, North Carolina.

1713

A number of villages had sprung up in the Schaharie Valley, the best known settlement in this region being "German

Flats," which was known far and wide as excellent farming country.

About seven hundred Palatine Germans moved on from the Schoharie Valley into the Mohawk Valley in upper New York State.

1714

In Skippack, Pennsylvania, the first great German-American pedagogue, Christopher Dock, began teaching. During his long career, he introduced the blackboard into the American schoolroom, and published in 1750, his Schulordnung, the first pedagogical work in America.

The first German settlement in Virginia was called Germanna. It was established as a result of Governor Alexander Spotswood's efforts to organize an iron works in the Virginia colony. Subsequently, a migration of eighty families from Württemberg settled in Madison County, Virginia.

1719

Between 6,000 and 7,000 Germans, popularly referred to as Palatines, but not all from the Palatinate, arrived in Philadelphia. They spread out into the Pennsylvania farm country.

1720

Beginning in 1720, and continuing for the next half century, an average of 2,000 Germans disembarked annually at ports along the Delaware. Many paid their own way, but most were compelled by their poverty to come as redemptioners, who unlike indentured servants, brought no formal indenture, but were bound by written agreements to pay fixed sums on arrival in the colonies. Being usually unable to do this, they were obliged to become servants in order to discharge the debt.

1721

The German redemptioner trade had become highly systemized with regulations prevailing both in the American colonies and Germany.

1722

Palatine scouts went into the valleys of Pennsylvania, and reported that the land between the Susquehanna and Schuylkill Rivers was good. Thirty three German families found their way to the eastern reaches of the Susquehanna River.

1723

Large segments of the Palatine Germans who had originally settled in New York State, continued to migrate. Following the original vanguard of a few German migrants, a large group moved into Bucks County, Pennsylvania, and five years later (1728) others entered Berks and Lebanon Counties in Pennsylvania.

1727

From 1727 on, German immigrants paid little attention to the efforts of other English colonies to attract them. Their land of Canaan was Pennsylvania. By 1727, the German population of Pennsylvania reached 20,000.

Germans from Pennsylvania crossed the Potomac River above Harper's Ferry, and founded New Mecklenburg, later renamed Shepardstown, Maryland.

1728

Germans began moving into Maryland, especially in and around the city of Baltimore. Another area of German settlement in Maryland was in the western counties, which received the overflow from Pennsylvania.

Conrad Beisel established the communitarian settlement of Dunkards at Ephrata, Pennsylvania. In its prime, the community had 300 members.

1729

Governor Robert Johnson of South Carolina established a series of German townships along the Carolina frontier with the dual purpose of guarding the frontier against Indian attacks, and helping to put down any slave uprisings.

1730

The German Reformed Church began establishing congregations and schools, and could point to many excellent scholars and organizers among its pastors. John Philip Boehm, George Michael Weiss, John Peter Miller, and Michael Schlatter were among those who made church history in America.

1732

A German-Swiss colony was established at Perrysburg, South Carolina to raise silk and cultivate vineyards. It lasted until the time of the American Revolution.

Benjamin Franklin, in order to capitalize on the large numbers of Germans in Pennsylvania, began publishing a German language newspaper, the Philadelphische Zeitung. It was badly edited in very poor German, and soon failed. Franklin also had financial interests in other German papers.

1733

German Seventh-Day Baptists established a school at Ephrata, Pennsylvania. Even from Philadelphia and Baltimore came young men seeking admission to the school.

Johann Peter Rockefeller went to work on a farm near Flemington, Hunterdon County, New Jersey. One of his descendents was John D. Rockefeller.

John Peter Zenger, who had arrived from Germany in 1710, opened the New York Weekly Journal in opposition to the arbitrary rule of Governor Cosby of New York.

1734

Twelve thousand Swiss-Germans emigrated to America in the decade from 1734 to 1744. Many of them founded communities in the South, while some went to the Palatine colony at New Bern, North Carolina.

Georgia had few non-English immigrants, but one group of Germans, the Salzburgers, founded Ebenezer, some 25 miles from Savannah. It was the most southerly of all German settlements in colonial America.

1735

South Carolina received a large contingent of German settlers who came into America through the port of Charleston. A few remained in the city, but most of them settled permanently in what was known as the Saxe-Gotha district, the present Orangeburg and Lexington Counties, then the extreme western frontier.

The first organized Lutheran Church in the Carolinas was the German church in Orangeburg, South Carolina.

Count Nicholas Ludwig von Zinzendorf, the leader of the evangelical sect, the Unitas Fratum or Moravians arrived in Savannah, Georgia, and established a settlement of Moravians in this area.

John Peter Zenger was tried for libel, and was defended by Andrew Hamilton of Philadelphia, who secured Zenger's acquittal. The case is a landmark in the history of the freedom of the press in America.

1736

A large group of German Moravians, who had originally settled in Georgia, moved to Pennsylvania, where, subsequently, they founded the towns of Bethlehem, Nazareth, and Lititz.

A German settlement was established at Waldoboro, Maine. It was named after a Pomeranian soldier, Samuel Waldo, who had earlier migrated to Boston, and had become involved in land speculation in Maine.

1738

Samuel Waldo returned to Germany, where he recruited forty families from Saxony and Brunswick to settle on his land in Maine. More German families soon followed.

1739

The Germantauner Zeitung, one of the first German language newspapers in America, began to be published in Germantown, Pennsylvania by Christopher Saur II.

Conrad Beisel, the founder of Ephrata in Pennsylvania, published a songbook of 692 songs, probably the first hymn book issued in America.

1740

A group of German Moravians, under the leadership of Johann Kelpius, established a communistic colony at Bethlehem, Pennsylvania. It was well known for the ability of its members to cast horoscopes and perform astrological feats.

From 1740 onward, the Germans cast their votes for the Quaker party in Pennsylvania, enabling the Quakers to control the affairs of the colony until 1756, even though they were a minority.

1741

By 1741, over 1,200 Salzburgers had settled in Georgia, and were receiving aid from German church groups in Halle and Augsburg, as well as some initial support from the British government.

Nicholas von Zinzendorf left the Moravian colony in Georgia with some of his followers and moved to Bethlehem, Pennsylvania.

1743

Four hundred German redemptioners set sail for Philadelphia. Only fifty survived the crossing to America. German immigrants did not receive a very cordial welcome in Philadelphia by this time. A dreaded disease in the city was termed "Palatine Fever," and a pesthouse was erected where all ships bearing German redemptioners were quarantined.

Christopher Saur II, printed the complete Lutheran Bible in the German language. It was the first Bible printed in a European language in the American colonies.

1745

The German population of Pennsylvania exceeded 45,000 people.

The German colonists founded the town of Frederick, Maryland, and shortly thereafter, Hagerstown was laid out by Jonathan Hagar, a Pennsylvania German.

A number of Germans from Waldoboro joined the punitive expedition of the British against the French fort of Louisburg on Cape Breton Island, Nova Scotia.

1746

April

The Waldoboro settlement was attacked by Indians, most of its inhabitants were killed, and all they had built was destroyed.

1747

Michael Schlatter, a German Reformed pastor, established the first German Reformed church in America.

1748

Reverend Henry Melchior Mühlenberg took the lead in promoting the formation of a Lutheran Synod, not only to further the work of the Lord in America, but to combat the irregularities and help overcome the difficulties which arose in churches widely scattered over the Pennsylvania German farming country.

1749

This was a peak year for German immigration, when over 6,000 emigrants from Württemberg, Zweibucken, Mannheim, the "Pfalz," and other German states found new homes in America.

1750

By 1750, the Germans had established an almost continuous string of back country settlements that ran all the way from the head of the Mohawk Valley in New York to Savannah, Georgia.

The Germans in New York State occupied a strip of territory some twelve miles long along the left bank of the Mohawk River.

Gottlieb Mittleberger, who came to America in 1750, wrote a book concerned with his Journey to Pennsylvania, which described in detail, the horrible conditions aboard the German immigrant ships.

By 1750, the Moravians had established thirteen schools in Lancaster, Berks, York, and Montgomery Counties in Pennsylvania. Americans from all over the colonies sent their children to the Moravians to be educated.

The Shenandoah Valley became the main avenue for the advance of the German element into Virginia and North Carolina.

1751

Sixteen vessels brought 4,134 German immigrants to Philadelphia. Some remained in the city, but the majority dispersed into the surrounding countryside.

By 1751, the most northerly German settlement was Waldoboro, Maine, which had been partially rebuilt after the Indian disaster five years earlier.

1753

A large group of Moravians moved into North Carolina, where they bought a huge tract of land. They named their settlement "Wachovia," and formed a prosperous communitarian colony.

May

Some Germans from the "Wachovia" colony established a settlement at Bethabara, North Carolina.

1754

The "Society for propagating Christian Knowledge Among the Germans in America" was organized in Philadelphia to help in assimilating and absorbing German immigrants into American life.

A German evening school was opened in Philadelphia to serve the needs of those colonists who could not attend classes during the day because of other committments.

The Schwenkfelders, a German sectarian group in Pennsylvania, were probably the best educated of all German immigrants. What was probably the first Sunday School, Die Kindlehr, was established by them in 1754.

1755

Zion's German Church was established in Baltimore, and is still thriving in the very center of Baltimore's business district.

By 1755, Moravian missionaries had been sent into the outlying frontier areas, and had established missions among the Indians. These missions extended as far west as Gnadenhutten, in the Ohio country.

July 9

The Germans of Pennsylvania and Maryland contributed heavily toward the successful conclusion of the French and Indian War. They provided the horses and wagons to carry the expedition of General James Braddock inland.

1756

Large numbers of nonsectarian Germans from Pennsylvania spilled over the southern borders of that province into Frederick County, Maryland. Barbara Fritchie, the heroine of John Greenleaf Whittier's famous poem, was named Barbara Hauer before her marriage. Her German parents had come to Maryland from Lancaster County, Pennsylvania. Other groups crossed the Delaware to enter and settle in Hunterdon and Mercer Counties, in New Jersey.

In the political controversies in Pennsylvania, the vast body of Germans usually continued to side with the Quaker party. For the Mennonites, Amish, and Dunkards, the teachings of George Fox had much in common with the founder of their sects, Menno Simons. However, in 1756, the Germans voted against the Quakers and with their Presbyterian Scotch-Irish neighbors, thereby wresting control of the colony from the Quakers.

1757

A French led force of Indians attacked the settlement of German Flats, New York, and killed forty men, women and children, and took about a hundred prisoners.

1758

Again in 1758, Indians attacked German Flats, but were driven off this time, by the settlers led by Nicholas Herkimer.

Christian Frederick Post, a Moravian missionary, went on a mission to the villages of the Indians along the Ohio River. He was able to induce the redmen to desert their French allies.

November 25   The Germans provided horses, wagons, and supplies, in addition to fighting with General John Forbes in his attempt to drive the French out of Fort Duquesne. One of the most effective military units engaged in the war was the Royal American Regiment, which was recruited, almost wholly, from German inhabitants of Pennsylvania and Maryland.

1759

By 1759, the "Society for Propagating Christian Knowledge Among the Germans in America," had established eight schools throughout the German settlements, and had extended aid to Lutheran and Reformed ministers who gave religious and secular instruction to German children.

A group of Schwenkfelders founded a settlement in New York, which they named Pen-Yan, a combination of the words Pennsylvania and Yankees.

1761

The first German-American academy was opened in Germantown, Pennsylvania.

1763

August 2   The Battle of Bushy Run ended the threat of Indian uprisings in Pennsylvania. It was fought in a German settlement in Westmoreland County, and the victors were the German soldiers of the Royal American Regiment under Colonel Henri Bouquet.

1764

By 1764, the German settlement at Saxe-Gotha, South Carolina had 600 German inhabitants. By 1850, it had lost all evidences of its German origin, except for the popularity of its German sausage, and Christmas Cakes.

The major portion of the German vote in the Pennsylvania election of 1764 was cast against the petition seeking a royal charter which would have turned Pennsylvania into a royal colony.

1765

At least forty Lutheran congregations in Pennsylvania, New York, New Jersey, Maryland and Virginia were reg-

ularly connected with and responsible to the synod established by Reverend Henry Melchior Mühlenberg.

1766

The German Friendly Society of Charleston was founded
with Michael Kalteisen as its first president. It was devoted to charitable and social purposes.

Benjamin Franklin told the British House of Commons that
one-third of the population of Pennsylvania was German.
Ten years later, the German population of Pennsylvania
numbered between 110,000 and 150,000.

1768

By 1768, Louisiana had a German coast, the Côte des
Allemands, extending on both sides of the Mississippi River above New Orleans, and occupied by a few hundred Germans. In the nineteenth century, thousands of Germans
arrived in New Orleans. Many did not proceed into the interior, but remained in the city forming a German quarter.

Lewis Wetzel, whose antecedents were Pennsylvania German, was second only to Daniel Boone in the pioneering
and settlement of early Kentucky.

1770

By 1770, more than 3,000 German Protestants had settled
in North Carolina, mostly of Pennsylvania German stock,
and Lutheran churches flourished in these German sections
of the Carolinas for many years.

1772

The Moravians founded the mission of Schönbrunn in Ohio.
John Heckewelder, David Zeisberger, and Christian Friedrich Post are the names of the Moravian missionaries who
were intimately connected with the early history of white
settlement in Ohio.

1773

The first German Lutheran Seminary was opened by the
Reverend John Christian Kunze, but was forced to close
when the American Revolution broke out.

The German governments, fearful of excessive population losses, were especially hostile to those Germans who had returned to the "Fatherland" from America as emigration agents. One German province decreed that repatriates would need permission to enter, and once granted, the individual was given a stipulated time to transact his business.

1774

June 1

The Closing of the Port of Boston Act particularly incensed the Germans. It reminded them of the dreaded Hussars who had burned and pillaged their homes and lands in the old country. The colonial Germans joined in the protests which were raised against these Intolerable Acts, and they helped to raise money for the relief of Boston.

1775

At the outbreak of the American Revolution, immigrants from the German states in Pennsylvania totaled 110,000 out of a population of 225,000, or almost one-half of the colony's population. Large groups of these Germans were designated as "Dutch," a corruption of the ancient word Deutsch meaning the "folk."

German settlers accounted for approximately ten percent of the total whole population of the thirteen colonies.

When the American Revolution began, the Germans tended to respond to the pressure of the environment to the exclusion of ties of common origin. In Pennsylvania and New York, they supported the Revolution, while in Georgia, most of them became Loyalists. There was a definate split among the colonial Germans in their support for the Revolutionary cause.

May

Charleston, South Carolina created a volunteer company after the Battles of Lexington and Concord known as the German Fusileers.

June

Four companies of German-American infantry were raised in Reading, Pennsylvania loyal to the American cause.

1776

At the time the colonies revolted, there were, 1,500 Germans in New England, 25,000 in New York, 110,000 in

Pennsylvania, 15,000 in New Jersey, 20,500 in Maryland and Delaware, 25,000 in Virginia, 8,000 in North Carolina, 15,000 in South Carolina, and 5,000 in Georgia.

By 1776, there were only 2,500 German Moravians in America, and they, and their fellow sectarians accounted for only a tiny fraction of the total German immigration.

While many ministers of the German Reformed Church openly supported the American Revolution, the German Lutheran clergy, with the notable exception of the Reverend Peter Mühlenberg, who became a Revolutionary General, were inclined to support the British.

May

The Continental Congress authorized a German regiment to be recruited in Pennsylvania and Maryland. Under the command of Nikalas Hausseger and Ludwig Weltner, these Germans saw service in a number of campaigns, especially those in New Jersey.

July

The Germantauner Zeitung under Christopher Saur III's proprietorship expressed loyalist and pacifist views during the Revolution.

July 5

Henry Miller, subsequently the printer for Congress, announced the ratification of the Declaration of Independence in his Staatsbote, a day ahead of the other Philadelphia newspapers, and issued a complete German translation of the Declaration on July 9, 1776.

August

The Continental Congress began to lure hired Hessian soldiers from their British allegiance by promising them all the rights of native Americans, in addition to fifty acres of land a piece for common soldiers, and much larger quotas for officers. Some 12,000 Hessians, subsequently, remained in the United States after the Revolution was ended.

1777

Maria Ludwig, known in Revolutionary War legends as "Molly Pitcher," was a German immigrant who lived in Carlisle, Pennsylvania, and participated in some of the battles in New Jersey.

Christopher Ludwig, a Pennsylvania German, was appointed director of baking for the Continental Army.

The patriarch of German Lutheranism in America, the Reverend Henry Melchior Mühlenberg, refused, at first, to take sides in the American Revolution. He later swore allegiance to the United States, but when the British occupied Philadelphia, Mühlenberg informed General William Howe that he had remained loyal to the king as long as circumstances had allowed.

General George Washington's personal bodyguards were a detachment of cavalry from Major F. Von Heer's Independent Troop of Horse recruited largely from Germans living in Pennsylvania and Maryland.

Two of Christopher Saur III's sons published in Philadelphia, the virulently anti-patriot journal, the Pennsylvanische Staats Courier.

July 23
When General Howe invaded and captured Philadelphia, the Liberty Bell was hauled down, and placed in the German church (Reformed) at Allentown, Pennsylvania for safe keeping.

August 6
General Nicholas Herkimer, led the German farmers of the Mohawk Valley in New York against the invading British, and Indians. At the battle of Oriskany, in which he was mortally wounded, Herkimer defeated the British forces, and cut off General John Burgoyne from supplies and relief from the West.

September 11
At the Battle of Brandywine Creek, two reliable German brigade commanders, Peter Mühlenberg and George Wieden, whose regiments were composed mainly of German settlers from the Valley of Virginia and elsewhere, distinguished themselves in a daring manuever that covered the retreat of the American Army, and prevented its annihilation by the British.

October 4
At the Battle of Germantown, Peter Mühlenberg led his German regiment in a brilliant bayonet charge which pierced the enemy's right wing.

1778

Sulphur and saltpeter, necessary ingredients for the manufacture of gunpowder, were obtained by the Revolutionary Armies from the German settlements along the Codouis Creek in York County, Pennsylvania.

April

The <u>Philadelphische Staatsbote</u>, published by Henry (Heinrich) Miller, was a violently anti-British newspaper from the time of the Stamp Act in 1765 onward, and except when the British seized his type and press in the Spring of 1778, he kept up a spirited newspaper war on the Saur family.

May 5

General Frederick William Steuben, drillmaster of the American forces, was appointed Inspector General of the Revolutionary Army by George Washington. He fought in a number of engagements, and when the war was over, von Steuben, which he preferred to be called, remained in the United States. Until his death, he was identified with all of his adopted country's military interests.

1781

October 19

When General Lord Cornwallis surrendered at Yorktown, it was von Steuben who planted the regimental standard on the British fortifications opposite the American positions.

1783

Five thousand Hessian soldiers who had fought for the British in the Revolutionary War, settled permanently in the United States at the war's conclusion. Most of them, subsequently, found their way to the German counties in Pennsylvania, New York and Virginia, and were quickly absorbed by the German communities in these areas.

Shortly after the end of the Revolutionary War, hundreds of immigrants of German stock joined the march through the mountain gaps and down the river valleys into Kentucky, Tennessee, and the new west.

September

The German Society of Maryland was founded.

1784

A <u>Deutsche Gesellschaft</u> was organized in New York City to help German immigrants on their arrival in America. German Revolutionary Army officers, such as Heinrich Emmanuel Lutter and General von Steuben, served as its presidents, and years later, John Jacob Astor, himself a German immigrant from Baden, willed $20,000 to the society.

1785

Drs. H. Schmidt and F. Helmuth opened a private seminary in Pennsylvania, which, during the next twenty years, prepared men for the German Lutheran ministry.

1786

Conrad Beisel's Ephrata community was incorporated under state law, and was managed by a board of trustees. The old rules of celibacy and the cloistered life were abandoned.

The first "pretention" concert, involving a large number of both vocal and instrumental performers, was given in the Reformed German Church of Philadelphia.

The Pennsylvania Legislature ordered its Journal and other official papers to be printed in German translation.

May 4   Philadelphia, with its large German population, developed the first classical music program in the United States.

1787

Franklin College at Lancaster, Pennsylvania was incorporated. It was originally intended to be a Pennsylvania German college, with the courses taught in German. Financial and language troubles hampered the institution from the beginning, and it was closed in 1821, reopened in 1839; and in 1850, included within the structure of Franklin and Marshall College.

1788

The German Quakers of Germantown, Pennsylvania issued a formal protest against the institution of Negro slavery, continuing the precedents set by the Germans in the seventeenth century.

1789

The Amish and Mennonite Germans of Pennsylvania played a leading role in the development of constructive farming, especially in regard to the use they made of grasses and meadows.

The British Consul at Philadelphia, Phineas Bond, reported that an almost total halt to German immigration had occurred. This was to be only a temporary condition.

April 1   Frederick Augustus Mühlenberg, the brother of Peter, became the first Speaker of the newly formed House of Representatives. He also served later as the third Speaker of the House.

1798

Gottlieb Graupner, a native of Hanover arrived in Boston. He is usually considered the father of orchestral music in the United States.

July 9   The German-American element violently denounced the passage of the Alien and Sedition Laws. In most states, they openly defied the laws, and in Pennsylvania, defiance flared into violence.

1799

February   John Fries, a Welshman, led a large group of Pennsylvania Germans, living in Northampton, Bucks and Montgomery Counties in an insurrection, known as Fries Rebellion, in opposition to the direct Federal property tax established by Congress. Fries was caught and the insurrection ended in Eastern Pennsylvania. Though not as violent, it was comparable to the insurrection of the Paxton Boys in that state.

1800

By 1800, foreign born ministers in the German churches began to be succeeded by men born and trained in the United States. In New York, Philadelphia, and the German counties of Maryland, Virginia, and North Carolina, numerous German congregations adopted English as the language of worship, though in many places only after violent conflict and even schism.

As early as 1800, there was a German music dealer in Lancaster, Pennsylvania, who imported musical compositions from a publisher in Leipzig, Germany.

December 3   German-Americans voted overwhelmingly for Thomas Jefferson for the presidency, and welcomed the coming of the new order. They found in Jefferson's interpretation of Democracy a consumation which they had long devoutly wished, and had therefore opposed the Federalist party in all of its actions.

ANTE-BELLUM IMMIGRATION-1801-1860

1801

The German Moravian missionaries founded their first
settlement in Ohio at Salem in Tuscarawas County. In
recent years, the state of Ohio has reconstructed the
early village of Schöenbrunn near New Philadelphia, Ohio,
and designated it a state park.

1802

The German community in Tuscarawas County, Ohio was
comprised of 300 pious, simple German peasants from
Wurtemberg.

1803

In 1803, Johann Georg Rapp, a religious communitarian,
purchased 5,000 good acres of land in Butler County, Pennsylvania. His followers, 600 strong came to America two
years later.

1805

Rapp's followers established themselves in a communitarian settlement at Harmony, Pennsylvania.

The German Pennsylvania Synods of the Lutheran and Reformed Churches sent itinerant ministers into Ohio to service the religious needs of the new German immigrants entering that region.

1807

Much of the German immigration went west, along the Erie
Canal to the Great Lakes, and thence to the prairies. Cincinnati had included prominent Germans in its population
since the beginning of the nineteenth century, and became
one of the leading German-American cities in the United
States. Martin Baum, a successful businessman became
the first German mayor of that city.

1808

George Michael Bedinger, a noted Kentucky pioneer, and a
man of German parentage, drew up a bill for the preven-
tion of the importation of Negro slaves into the United
States after 1808.

1811

Friedrich Ludwig Jahn, "Vater Jahn," as he was called, established his first Turnplatz in Berlin. This was the beginning of the Turnvereine whose idealism actuated much of the leadership of the German immigration. The basic principle was "the healthy mind in the healthy body" concept.

1812

Simon Synder was elected Governor of Pennsylvania. In fact, twelve of the twenty seven governors of Pennsylvania from 1787 to 1942 were of colonial German ancestry.

1815

By 1815, Philadelphia, New York, and Baltimore, which had had formerly two or three German-language newspapers a piece, could not boast one among them. Only in the small towns of the Pennsylvania-German country, like Allentown, Lancaster, and Reading, did they survive. The situation would change considerably with the influx of Germans during the 1840's and 1850's.

In Pennsylvania, the public use of the German language was decidedly on the wane. However, German lingered on as the language of the home, especially in remote regions as late as 1900.

Boston's Germans founded the Handel and Haydn Society.

Only the churches of the Pennsylvania-German country had made no concession to the use of English in the church service.

The Rappist colony in Pennsylvania moved to Indiana, and built New Harmony, about fifty miles from the mouth of the Wabash River. There, the community thrived under the leadership of Friedrich Rapp, an adopted son of Johann Georg Rapp.

1817

By 1817, the Würtembergers in Tuscarawas County, Ohio had built a blockhouse.

Joseph Baumeler led a group of German Separatists into Ohio to found a communitarian settlement called Zoar.

1818

German intellectuals in the Old Country proposed colonization schemes which would concentrate the Germans going to the United States in one geographical area, so that
all the cultural advantages of the homeland might be preserved.

1819

March

Congress adopted a Passenger Act which finally put an end
to the German redemptioner trade.

April 15

More than 150 Würtembergers in Tuscarawas County, Ohio,
signed an agreement establishing communism in their community. This agreement was reinforced in 1824, when
another group signed the covenant.

1820

The government of Prussia made it a crime to urge emigration, and at a later date even forbade the reading of letters
or papers which might induce such action.

1823

February

The first all German singing society was organized in Cincinnati.

1824

December 1

Although the Germans, as a group, voted for Andrew Jackson for president, their vote does not appear to have been
decisive in this election.

1825

Because of malaria in Indiana and trouble with meddlesome
neighbors, the entire community of New Harmony moved
back to Economy, Pennsylvania. Robert Owen, the great
Scottish Utopian Socialist, bought out the community in
Indiana.

Several thousand Germans emigrated to Brazil, believing
that the best opportunities in the United States had been
seized. This movement to Brazil continued throughout the
1820's.

1826

The first German newspaper in Cincinnati was established. It was a weekly, Die Ohio Chronik.

1828

As a result of a discriminatory series of laws passed in Bavaria, and Würtemberg, against Jews of German origin, a veritable exodus of tradespeople and professionals took place. Their destination was America.

December 3

German-Americans, as a group, regarded Andrew Jackson as the champion of a great cause. They voted for him for the presidency, and in Berks County, Pennsylvania, it was said that the Germans were still voting for Andrew Jackson long after he was dead.

1829

Gottfried Duden, who had spent three years in Missouri, returned to Germany, and wrote a book which described everyday living on an American farm in idyllic terms. The book acted as a great propaganda agent in favor of emigration.

1830

Two ships left Hamburg, Germany crowded with emigrants. One reached Rio De Janeiro, and the other landed at New Orleans, its German passengers proceeding up the Mississippi River to the farmlands of Missouri.

Union County, Ohio, an excellent agricultural area attracted a large German Lutheran farming population from Bavaria, and Hess-Darmstadt beginning in 1830.

A group called the Dreissiger, that emigrated after the political disturbances of 1830 in Germany, included such intellectuals as Gustav Körner, Judge J. Bernhard Stallo, Dr. Konstantin Hering, Dr. Oswald Seidensticker, Friedrich Munch, Friedrich Theodor Engelmann, George Bunsen, and Wilhelm Weber.

Most of the German immigration was a matter of individuals seeking new opportunities, but there were also a number of colonization companies to promote the settlement of particular areas. All of these attempts failed. The

earliest of these companies was the Giessener Auswinder-
ungs Gesellschaft which included a number of university
men, and planned to settle a German state in Arkansas.
Some of the others were the Rhein-Bayerische Gesellschaft,
and the Mainzer Adelsverein, which was interested in the
development of Texas.

1831

The American Consul at Frankfort-on-Main reported that
because of the encouraging letters of earlier German immigrants, the emigrating passion had become more general
especially among middle class people.

The most distinguished leader of the Germans in Charleston, South Carolina, was Johann Andreas Wagener, who
came to the United States in 1831. He was prominent in
every activity of the German group, as well as in all civic
affairs.

German immigrants began to come to Buffalo in large numbers, and by the end of the decade, an influential German
element had been added to the original New England strain
in that city.

1832

By 1832, German immigration to the United States exceeded
10,000; by 1834, 17,000; by 1837, 24,000; and from 1845 to
the outbreak of the Civil War, 1,250,000. The primary
cause of German immigration was undoubtedly economic,
although the disturbed political conditions of western Europe played a part as well.

Bremen was the chief port of departure for German immigrants going to America. In 1832, the Bremen city government passed regulations to make the port a safer place
for emigrants.

Heinrich Koch, a German radical, migrated to Iowa, and
founded a colony of Fourierites in Clayton County, Iowa,
near Dubuque. It went the way of all Utopian experiments
in America, largely as a result of difficulties over land
titles.

The Würtemberger colony in Ohio was incorporated as the "Separatist Society of Zoar." Joseph Baumeler who had founded the colony in 1817, continued as its leader until his death in 1853.

December 5   Although Henry Clay and the Whig party tried to woo the German vote in the presidential election, the German affiliation with the Democratic party continued, and they cast their ballots once again for Andrew Jackson.

1833

The German advance up the Missouri River was well under way by this year.

The Giessener Gesellschaft attempted to mass German immigrants along the Missouri River near St. Louis for the purpose of establishing a purely German colony in the state of Missouri.

Dr. Georg Engelmann came to St. Louis. He was a chemist, and geologist, in addition to being a practicing physician. He helped found the Western Academy of Science in St. Louis.

German immigrants in Missouri, writing home, begged for German song books and musical compositions.

1834

German immigrants, even university products, handled picks and shovels in building the Schuykill Canal.

The organization of German Catholic parishes followed rapidly on the heels of German immigration. German Catholics at Minster and Glandorf, Ohio, completed the organization of their churches.

Friedrich Rapp died, and the settlement at Economy, Pennsylvania was guided by a council of nine elders, who were chosen to run the spiritual life of the community.

The first political demonstration of German-Americans against nativism occurred in New York City.

By 1834, the German Reformed Church was maintaining 160 schools, and the German Lutheran church 250 schools.

By far the most influential German language newspaper in the United States was the New Yorker Staats-Zeitung. Its broad democratic sympathies appealed to workingmen, and its vigorous editorials supported the Democratic party. It was capably owned and managed by G. A. Neumann.

1835

There were numerous German singing societies in the United States. One of the most famous, the Philadelphia Männerchor, was founded in this year.

Germans were especially important in the spread of homeopathy in the United States. Dr. Wilhelm Wesselhoft, and Dr. Konstantin Hering were the founders of the North American Academy of Homeopathic Healing Art, established in Allentown, Pennsylvania.

St. Louis, Missouri, had, by this date, a fairly large German element, centered largely in the southern part of the city. The first German newspaper in St. Louis was the Anzeiger des Westens, and ten years later, the city had two German dailies.

As early as 1835, the Germans were the second largest immigrant group in New York City. They were scattered throughout the commercial districts of the lower wards, and the Tenth Ward was so densely populated with Germans that it was known as "Kleindeutschland."

1836

American consuls in Germany reported that, while paupers and even criminals were being regularly shipped out of various German towns and communes to the United States, only a few hundred undesirables were annually involved.

Of all the non-Lutheran Protestant sects, the Methodists were more interested in the German immigrants than any other religious denomination. In 1836, the Ohio Annual Conference of Methodists appointed William Nut to a German mission on a central Ohio circuit, where he traveled from German settlement to German settlement. He also translated the Methodist catechism and discipline into German.

The first German-English school west of the Mississippi was founded in St. Louis, and Friedrich Steines was called from his Missouri farm to become its teacher.

Daniel Schlesinger of Hamburg opened a music school in New York City. German music teachers did so much to develop American interest in music in the nineteenth century, that much of our musical terminology today is German rather than English or Italian.

The diocese of New York and half of New Jersey contained about 200,000 Catholics, and of the 38 priests only three were German. This was to cause difficulties later on in the nineteenth century.

As early as 1836, Cleveland, Ohio had German churches, and societies.

Germans in Pennsylvania opposed that state's first common school laws, as they disapproved of education for the masses, and the payment of taxes to support other people's children in schools.

1837

Steerage passage for German immigrants coming to America from Bremen was $16.

Friedrich Froebel, who established the first kindergarten in Blankenburg, Germany, became the great pedagogue, whose methods were widely used in the United States by Germans and non-Germans alike.

Johann Martin Henni founded the first German Catholic Orphans Society in the United States in Cincinnati, and he later became the first German Catholic Bishop in this country.

A Pennsylvania statute of 1837, and an Ohio law of the same year permitted not only the teaching of German in the public schools, but teaching in German as well, whenever there was sufficient demand for it.

The Pennsylvania Legislature began publishing its laws, and the governor's messages in German translation.

The town of Hermann, Missouri was laid out by German immigrants in the midst of the Panic of 1837, but managed to survive. It was destined to become one of the most important German cultural centers in America.

A German sharpshooter company was organized in New Orleans. In the same year, a Deutscher Liederkranz began to sing German songs in the city.

The Baltimore Liederkranz (singing society) was organized, and began giving concerts.

A call was issued for a convention of all Germans in the United States to discuss plans for preserving the German language in America, to promote a German press, normal schools for the training of German teachers, and a German university. These conventions were actually held in 1837, 1838, and 1839, but accomplished very little.

1838

The Methodist Church in America voted financial support for German immigrants, and founded a German Methodist newspaper in Cincinnati. The Methodists also began sending missionaries to the cities of the East coast to meet incoming German immigrants.

A German Catholic congregation was founded in Louisville, Kentucky, the first of its kind in that state.

The first male chorus of Cincinnati Germans met at an inn in the German section of the city known as "Over the Rhine."

Among the religious malcontents who left Germany were the followers of Martin Stephan, a religious mystic of Dresden.

August 11   German newspapers in the United States were anti-European especially anti-British and Irish on the whole. The Summeytown Bauernfreund warned that, "If more Irish come into our country, the English and the Irish will rule over us Americans."

1839

Theodore Bernhard organized the school system of Watertown, Wisconsin, and introduced the first system of free text books in that state.

Hermann, Missouri had grown to a population of 450. Its settlers turned mainly to the cultivation of grapes, and its wine earned a nationwide reputation.

.1840

Concordia College in Indiana was established by German
Lutherans.   Indiana had an especially strong German section in and around Fort Wayne.

Germans felt particularly at home in Wisconsin. The
heaviest German immigration into that state began in 1840,
and lasted until the outbreak of the Civil War.

The number of German communities in the Southern states
is surprising in view of the general assumption that all German immigrants avoided the South because of slavery.   In
1840, the Germans of Richmond, Virginia celebrated their
first Volksfest in honor of Johannes Gutenberg.

By 1840, the German vote of Pennsylvania was regarded as
very important, and campaign biographies of Martin Van
Buren, and William Henry Harrison appeared in the German
language.

In Louisville, Kentucky, a semi-weekly German language
newspaper was established.

The linen industry of western Germany reached a crisis
as a result of the introduction of power looms, and whole
families of spinners and weavers sold their lands and emigrated to America on the proceeds.

Beginning in 1840, the "Old Lutheran" Germans from Saxony, who were ultra-conservative in their views, arrived in
the United States, and the battle against liberal and pietis-
tic influences in the German Church in America was initia-
ted.

German immigrants, who moved into the frontier areas
urged evangelical unity.   This view was exemplified by the
Deutsche Evangelische Kirshenverein des Westens, which
was organized in 1840, and whose members adhered strictly to the scriptures.

By 1840, the Germans were well established in Cincinnati.
Many owned vineyards and were engaged in trade and industry, such as the jewelry business and the manufacture of
stoves and musical instruments.   The German penetration
and concentration in Cincinnati, led to the development of
the famous "Over-the-Rhine" district, an area across the
Ohio canal where the Germans settled, and which became
a miniature "Deutschland."

1841

Many Germans in Mobile, Alabama organized the Freund-schaftbund to promote literary and benevolent activities among the German population living there.

C. F. W. Walther, the leader of the "Old Lutheran" sect, founded the first German Lutheran Church in St. Louis. He established a church journal, Der Lutheraner, and later organized the very powerful Missouri Synod as a reaction against the Americanized Lutheran Church of colonial days.

Franz Joseph Grund, a Bohemian German intellectual, and a member of the Turnverein in America, received a consul's post as a reward for writing campaign biographies for the Whig party.

Heinrich Adam Ginal, a German Lutheran preacher in Pennsylvania, founded a free rationalist congregation in Philadelphia.

A German teacher's seminary was opened, but soon collapsed, because of a lack of funds, and also because it was dominated by German liberals, whose unorthodox views offended German Lutherans and Catholics.

September 3 — German militia companies proved more popular than fire-fighting organizations. In Philadelphia, the Germans had a whole brigade, consisting of artillery, infantry, and rifle corps. German militia companies were formed in many cities, such as Cincinnati, Louisville, Columbus, New York, Chicago, and Milwaukee.

September 7 — The German Society of Maryland cared for the needs of the German immigrant passengers stricken with typhus aboard the ship Virginia, and paid all the medical bills amounting to $400.

1842

Charleston, South Carolina had a German population of 1,200, with two military companies, a German fire company, and a German literary society.

To counteract the appeal of lodges and beneficent societies, such as the free-masons, and to provide greater cohesion among Germans of the Catholic faith, the Deutsch-Römish

Katholischer Zentralverein was organized.

Iowa had few Germans until the Cincinnati Deutscher West-lich Ansiedlungs Verein settled the town of Gettysburg in 1842. Later strong German communities developed in and around Davenport.

A German newspaper, Der Deutsche Courier, made its first appearance in New Orleans. The owners were Alfred Schucking and Joseph Cohn, a German-Jew.

Several members of a German pietist sect founded by Michael Krausert, Barbara Heinemann, and Christian Metz came to the United States. The advance guard consisted of Metz, G. A. Weber, Wilhelm Noe, and G. Ackermann, who bought 5,000 acres of old Seneca, Indian Reservation Lands near Buffalo, New York at $10 an acre. Six villages were built by 800 immigrants who came over shortly thereafter.

A complaint arose among native workingmen in New York City, that an influx of German tailors, shoemakers, and cabinet makers had lowered wages and deprived Americans of work.

July 12

Immigrant travel was not always romantic or safe. In 1842, German immigrants going up the Mississippi River to the mid-west from New Orleans, were severely injured when the flue of a Mississippi River boat collapsed. Ninety-five Germans were hurt in the accident.

1843

The German pietists at Buffalo drew up a constitution, "approved by the Lord," whereby everything except clothing and household good was to be held in common. A council of elders governed the settlements, and a board of sixteen trustees held title to the property for the community.

March

Six hundred German Inspirationists under the leadership of Christian Metz moved into the pietist settlements near Buffalo. Later, they would move to Amana, Iowa to establish a communitarian colony.

1844

Johann Martin Henni was appointed the first German Catholic Bishop of Milwaukee. In 1875, he was created an Arch-Bishop.

The first German newspaper in Illinois, Theodor Engelmann's Belleviller Beobachter appeared.

Wilhelm Keil founded a communitarian society colony at
Bethel, Missouri, which consisted of Germans who had
been resident in the United States for some time.

Based on a communal scheme proposed by Heinrich Adam
Ginal, a German worker's organization of 300 members
was created. Each member deposited his savings, and
a capital stock of $20,000 was accumulated. With this
amount, 30,000 acres were bought in McKean County,
Pennsylvania, and the settlements of Teutonia and Ginals-
burg were established. In this colony of German workers,
no one was to use cash.

August Waldauer came to St. Louis, where for twenty years
he directed the Beethoven Conservatory, and various other
musical societies.

Beginning in 1844, the Adelsverein, a colonization society
founded by a group of German princes and noblemen, attempted to send thousands of Germans to Southwest, Texas
in the hope of Germanizing that section of the state. The
effort continued until 1847.

July 4   The Germans of Columbus, Ohio, celebrating Independence
Day, wakened the city with cannon fire discharged by two
German artillery companies, who kept up a steady cannon-
ade until noon. American holidays were sometimes more
enthusiastically celebrated by the early German immigrants than by their American neighbors.

1845

Five hundred German farmers were settled at Bethel,
Missouri, and all property was held in common. Wilhelm
Keil's own brand of Methodism was practised.

Gustav Körner settled in the German community of Bell-
ville, St. Clair County, Illinois, where in 1845, he became
a judge on the Illinois Supreme Court.

Some places in Ohio in the nineteenth century, that had a
strong German element, were hardly touched by the German immigration of the ante-bellum decades. They trace
their German ancestry back to Pennsylvania-German migrants. These places include Canton, Massilon, Steuben-
ville, and Germantown which had five German churches.

New Braunfels, Texas was established because of the activities of a colonization society known as the Mainzer Adelsverein. Other German communities in Texas also date back to the period before the Civil War. In general, the German settlements of western Texas were distinguished by a more intensive agriculture, and by a large diversification of crops and occupations.

Wartburg, a German settlement promoted by a colonization company in eastern Tennessee, in 1845 had attracted 800 settlers.

New York City was the center of the early German labor movement in America; however, German labor agitation spread wherever German workers settled. Hermann Kriege founded the first German Workers Organization in the United States in New York City. It was called the Bund der Gerichten. From this association sprang the Deutsche Jung-Amerike Gemeinde (German Young America Community) which championed the demands of the American land reformers. The German labor organizations paralleled the American, and gave a radical, socialist turn to the labor movement in America.

A German reading club was opened in New York City, with Samuel Ludvigh as its president.

1846

Beginning in 1846, mass German emigration to the United States took place. By 1854, almost 900,000 Germans had arrived in America, and this figure outdistanced all other immigrant groups.

Maximilian Schaefer of Wetzlar, Germany, established a brewery in Milwaukee. It was one of the first of the great German lager beer establishments in America. Several other German breweries were opened during the succeeding years.

Because of the potato famines, and other economic hardships, German emigration was so large that emigrants without tickets were warned not to come to Bremen.

To a lesser degree than the Irish, the Germans also figured in the history of volunteer firefighting in the pre-Civil War days. The Franklin Spritzen Compagnie of St. Louis was organized.

The first attempt to create a German theater in Cincinnati was made by Christian Thielmann. His wife, Louise, was the leading actress.

The St. Louis Oratorio Society was founded by a German organist from Mühlhausen.

By 1846, there were three German singing societies in Cincinnati, enough to hold a small Sängerfest.

The German Worker's settlements in Pennsylvania failed with a loss of $40,000, owing to internal friction, and the failure to provide all that was needed for the support of the community. Similar attempts were made to establish German worker's colonies at Germania, Wisconsin, and Helvetia, Missouri, the latter settlement under the leadership of Andreas Dietsh.

The Adoptiv-Bürger, published in Philadelphia, was the first German Worker's newspaper to appear in the United States. It was run by German communists, who used it as a propaganda sheet.

February

A German Sängerfest (competitive singing by German singing societies) was held in Philadelphia.

March

A Turnverein and a German Masonic lodge were organized in Charleston, South Carolina. German artisans and workmen contributed greatly to the life of the city and were highly respected.

April 25

Clashes between the Irish, and the generally more peaceful Germans were frequent, stemming from divergences in customs and speech, but mainly because of economic rivalries. German laborers competed for employment with the Irish in the cities, the canals, and on the railroads. Germans were frequently used as strikebreakers, as at the Atlantic Dock strike in 1846 in Brooklyn, where Irish dock workers battled it out with a group of freshly landed Germans who were being used as scab laborers.

May

Forty young men from Darmstadt went to Texas to establish a German socialist colony. The colony failed almost immediately. It had been named Bettina, in honor of Bettina von Arnim, the literary friend of Johan Wolfgang von Goethe.

1847

The first group of Russian-Germans came to grow grapes on Kelly's Island, Ohio, and to farm in Iowa.

For much of the nineteenth century, Germans were the second largest Catholic group in America. As early as 1847, the German Catholics of Chicago were asking for a Coadjutor Bishop of their own nationality, though their diocese was only three years old.

There were several German congregations of free-thinkers located in Philadelphia, New York, Milwaukee, St. Louis, and Boston.

The first national convention of German workingmen was held in Philadelphia. It was greatly interested in the founding of worker's colonies, based on the Wilhelm Weitling pattern of a "republic of the toilers," but the only actual attempt made to put these theories into practice was the colony of Communia, in Clayton County, Iowa.

Among its founders were the survivors of Andreas Dietsh's Helvetia colony, and Heinrich Koch, a radical German watchmaker of St. Louis, who edited a radical paper, the Anti-Pfaff.

The New York Liederkranz, a German singing society, was founded.

The Germans found it easy to cross the East River and settle in Brooklyn. A closely knit German community was established in the Williamsburg section, comprising nearly two-thirds of the population in that area.

By 1847, more than 30,000 Germans had established themselves in Jersey City, and Hoboken, New Jersey, which became the "most German" of all cities in that state.

Wilhelm Weitling, the radical labor reformer from Magdeburg, Germany, finally arrived in the United States. Under his guidance, a secret organization, the Befreiungsbund (League of Deliverance) appeared in New York City, and in other German communities as far away as New Orleans, and New Braunfels, Texas.

Under the leadership of C. F. W. Walther, known as the
"Lutheran Pope of the West," the more recently arrived
German Lutheran immigrants broke away from the tradi-
tional German Lutheran Church, and organized the more
conservative, rival Missouri Synod.

1848

A number of colleges were established by the descendents
of the German colonists of the eighteenth century. Muhlen-
berg College in Allentown, Pennsylvania was founded, and
named in honor of Henry Melchior Mühlenberg, the patriarch of German Lutheranism in America. Other colleges
such as Albright, Gettysburg, Lebanon Valley, and Susquehanna were largely Pennsylvania German in personnel.

Stimulated by political refugees from abroad, the Germans
of New York City, and elsewhere, held mass meetings, at-
tended benefits, and joined societies for the collection of
money, and the dispatch of republican emigres to aid the
German revolutionists of 1848-1849.

The Germania Orchestra, one of the most important organizations in the development of American orchestral music,
was founded in New York City. Its nucleus was composed
of Carl Zerrahn, Carl Bergmann, William Schultze, and
Carl Sentz.

A German theater guild began presenting plays in Hermann,
Missouri on Sundays, and these presentations continued until 1866 without interruption.

John Jacob Astor, born at Waldorf, near Heidelberg, and
who had come to America in 1783, donated $400,000 to found
the Astor Library in New York City. He laid the founda-
tions of a great fortune by his monopoly of the fur trade in
the nineteenth century.

October   Of all the organizations introduced into the United States by
the German immigrants, none represented a higher level
of intellectual interest or broader cultural objectives than
the Turnverein. The most successful of these societies
was founded in Cincinnati in the fall of 1848, under the
leadership of Friedrich Hecker. Turner Societies, thereafter sprang up in many American cities. In Boston, the
chief organizer was Karl Heinzin; in New York, it was Gustav Struve; in Milwaukee, August Willich was the center of

the group.   The basic objective of the organization was the
development of a physical education program.

1849

Small groups of German "Forty Eighters" began arriving
in the United States after the failure of the Revolutions in
the Germanies.

Wilhelm Weitling founded an Arbeiterbund (Worker's
League) with a central organization in New York City.
This new association was dedicated to Weitling's Utopian
Socialist theories, and to the founding and support of "Communia," a communistic colony in Wisconsin, where German
immigrants were already flocking.   Neither the League or
the colony was ever successful, the League never having
more than a thousand members, the colony disintegrating
in 1853.   Nevertheless, Weitling was the most dominant
personality in the German labor movement during the first
half of the nineteenth century.

The first German Sängerbund (Organization of Singing
Societies) was launched in Cincinnati.

Eberhard Faber, of Nuremberg, came to New York, and
established the pencil business which has perpetuated his
name.

Heinrich Koch's title to land at the Communia Colony was
bought for $600, and he moved on to Dubuque, where he
became a politician, and dealt in government contracts.

The well-known Louisville Anzeiger, which had a long history extending into the twentieth century, was established
as a daily newspaper.

The Germania Orchestra began to make tours and gave
829 concerts between 1849-1854.

The Methodist Missionary Society reported 6,350 church
members in the German field, with nearly 100 churches
and 83 regular mission circuits.   Wilhelm Nast, and
Heinrich Bahm were the guiding spirits of German Methodism in America.

Dr. Abraham Jacobi, an outstanding "Forty-Eighter,"
opened the first free clinic for children's diseases in the
United States, and was a pioneer in infant feeding.

1850

By 1850, The German element in the United States constituted twenty-six percent of the total foreign born population.

Larger groups of "Forty-Eighters" began arriving. The greater majority of them went west. Among these new arrivals were a number of men of distinction, including, Karl Heinzen, Freidrich Hecker, Friedrich Hassaurek, Bernhard Domschke, Heinrich Börnstein, George Schneider, Lorenz Brentano, Herman Raster, Wilhelm Rapp, Casper Butz, Reinhold Solger, Emil Praetorius, Oswald Ottendorfer, Gustav Struve, and the greatest German-American of them all, Carl Schurz.

At Mainz, Germany, and in towns of the southern German states, brokers from Hamburg, Bremen and La Havre competed for immigrant business, sending agents along the main routes to meet emigrants, advertising in local newspapers, or enlisting the aid of local tradesmen or innkeepers.

The first Turner Hall in the United States was dedicated in Cincinnati. Thereafter, a national publication, known as Die Turnzeitung was established.

The Milwaukee Musikverein, organized in 1843, gave its first concert.

By 1850, life among the German element in Ohio was in full bloom. Columbus, Cleveland, Dayton, and other Ohio cities had sizeable and important German sections.

Some German groups rejected the idea of a church or congregation altogether. They were the freethinkers, or as they called themselves, the Freimännerverein. Friedrich Hassaurek began its organization in Cincinnati, from whence it spread to Indianapolis, Cleveland, Trenton, Galveston, Chicago, St. Louis and other cities.

By 1850, Milwaukee had become a thoroughly Germanized city. German was spoken on the streets, and bock beer, lager beer, and Maiwein were extensively advertised.

There were 2,000 Germans employed in the more technical phases of industry in Boston and its vicinity, and several hundred more scattered throughout the factory towns of the Connecticut Valley.

Schiller Festivals were held by German-Americans in Chicago and Belleville, Illinois.

Franz Arnold, a disciple of Wilhelm Weitling, attempted to spread Weitlings socialistic ideas in Philadelphia, St. Louis, Pittsburgh, and other western cities. They did not catch on with any real success.

By 1850, a German ghetto had developed in New York City's Tenth, Eleventh and Thirteenth Wards, known as Klein-deutschland. Until the Civil War, it contained about two thirds of New York's Germans. Here, the English language was rarely heard, and there was scarcely a business which was not run by Germans. Here also were to be found German churches, schools, restaurants, a Volks-theater, and a lending library. But what most attracted the attention of visitors was the number of beer saloons. On Sundays, particularly, these establishments were filled to overflowing, it being the common practice for the people to go from the inn to church and then return to the inn again. This was the "Continental Sunday," and it aroused great disfavor among natives, who followed the practices of the "American Sunday."

April 11	The first successful German Whig newspaper was established in New York City in 1850, in spite of that city's large German population who usually voted Democratic.
April 15	German cabinet makers, fringe-makers and button makers advertised in the local press in New York for members to join their newly organized union.
April 27	Horace Greeley's New York Tribune supported the German artisans in their efforts to organize the various trades into labor unions.
October 14	A German Teacher's Association was formed in New York City, by 25 of these professionals.

1851

Emmanuel Leutze, painted "Washington Crossing the Delaware, and "Westward Ho" for the national capitol. Other German painters of distinction have been William Ritschel, Carl Rungius, F. Winold Russ, Joseph Lauber, Karl Buehr, Joseph Leyendecker.

Wilhelm Weitling visited his old friends at Communia, and the colony became part of his Arbeiterbund, although there were only fifteen members at the time.

Joseph Wedemeyer, often called the most prominent German labor agitator in America during the first half of the nineteenth century, arrived in the United States. He was a Marxist who tried to spread a more radical type of activity among American workingmen. He founded a revolutionary society called the Proletarierbund, which attempted to combine political and industrial organization.

The first Turnverein in the State of Illinois was organized in Peoria and Chicago.

Many of the "Forty-Eighters" raised money for Gottfried Kinkel, a hero of the Revolution of 1848, who toured America, with the foolhardy expectation that Germany was ripe for another revolution, and that the political exiles would soon be able to return to the fatherland to help give the death blow to tyranny and oppression.

The all-time peak year for German immigration was 1851, when 221,253 persons arrived in the United States. It must be emphasized, that while the "Forty Eighters" constituted the most dynamic and well known group of German immigrants, the bulk of the newcomers emigrated not for political, but economic reasons.

New Orleans attracted its quota of German liberals, and a society was formed in Louisiana to further the democratization of Germany.

Johann August Roebling, an engineer from Thuringia, who had come to the United States in 1831, constructed the railroad suspension bridge at Niagara Falls, New York.

Bad blood existed between the "Grays" German intellectuals who came to the United States before 1848, and the "Greens," those German intellectuals who had come after 1848. Gustav Körner was the leader of the "Grays". The "Greens" refused to recognize the cultural achievements of their predecessors.

The port of Bremen created a Bureau of Information for immigrants going to America, so as to protect them from the exploitation of unscrupulous porters and hotel owners.

Karl Heinzen, one of the foremost names of the German press, began publishing the Deutsche Zeitung. He also published several other newspapers including Jonus (1852), the Schnellpost (1848), and the Pionier (1845), which he started in Cincinnati; brought to New York in 1854, and moved to Boston in 1859. All of his newspapers were organs of reform.

Karl Hassaurek became editor of the radical German-American newspaper, the Cincinnati Volksblatt.

1852

A large part of the German influx to America in the late 1840's and early 1850's was comprised of German-Jews. In 1852, a considerable number of this group arrived including such prominent men as Solomon Loeb, Jacob H. Schiff, Benjamin Altman, Julius Rosenwald, Otto H. Kahn, Adolphe S. Ochs, and others. The German-Jews were primarily an urban people who settled in the great cities of America.

A shipload of Germans disembarked at Boston, but marched across the city to the trains that were to take them West, flaunting a sign which bore the inscription: "Hail Columbia, Land of the Free. We Will Be No Burden to Massachusetts."

As early as 1852, some German-American leaders were beginning to manifest their displeasure with the Democratic party because of the latter's close identification with the slavery interests.

November 2

German-Americans seemed to have split their votes in the presidential election of 1852, some going for the Whig candidate Winfield Scott, while others remained staunchly in the Democratic camp, and cast their ballots for Franklin Pierce. In any case, their vote was not decisive.

Gustav Köerner was elected Lieutenant Governor of Illinois.

1853

Peak German immigration to the United States in the antebellum years was the 1853-1854 period when a total of 356,955 German emigrants came to America during these two years.

Oswald Ottendörfer bought the very influential German newspaper, the New Yorker Staats-Zeitung.

The first Texas Sängerfest was held in New Braunfels, and a German convention was held in San Antonio during the following year.

The beer gardens in Milwaukee were disliked by the native Americans, and the struggle between the adherents of the "American Sunday" and the "Continental Sunday" was especially heated in this city.

So heavy was the influx of German Catholics, and so rapid the establishment of German parishes that there were protests from German Catholics against the practice of sending Irish priests to minister to their religious needs; the demand for bishops and priests of their own nationality increased with the years.

By 1853, the North American Turnerbund included sixty societies scattered throughout the United States, but primarily located in the major cities.

In New Orleans, the German residents held a Volks-und-Schützenfest; a march of all social and benevolent societies, with bands playing and American and German flags carried aloft, to a park where games and shooting contests were held.

March 21   A general meeting of the New York German trades was held at Mechanics Hall, with the purpose of forming a workingmen's alliance. It was instigated by Joseph Wedemeyer, who formed out of it the Amerikanischer Arbeiterbund. Very little progress was made by this organization among the workers in and outside of New York.

June 6   Dozens of German immigrants after arrival in New York City, had no means of employment. The New York Times reported that they hung around the German boarding houses in Greenwich Street, or settled down in the Eleventh Ward to become peddlars and ragpickers.

June 11   The "Continental Sunday" versus the "American Sunday" question always caused difficulties. In Newark, New Jersey, 10,000 Germans petitioned the city council for a repeal of the Sunday laws prohibiting the sale of alcoholic beverages. Demonstrations of this sort helped to provoke nativist outbursts against German immigrants.

1854

This was another peak year for German immigration, when 215,000 newcomers arrived. Nineteen thousand of them remained in New York, but the larger majority pushed westward to Ohio, Illinois, Michigan and Wisconsin.

The New York Philharmonic Orchestra was bitterly attacked by nativists for playing only the music of German masters.

The German Congress of Freethinkers assembled at Cincinnati; there, resolutions were adopted condemning legal oaths, Sunday closing law, religious exercises in public schools, slavery, and capital punishment. The Congress supported homesteads, and inheritance taxes.

By 1854, the pietist community at Buffalo, New York, needed more land. Committees explored the west, and decided to buy land in Iowa.

The German Stadttheater was opened in New York City under competent German direction. Other German theaters were opened and maintained in Philadelphia, St. Louis, Chicago, Cincinnati, Milwaukee and San Francisco until the outbreak of World War I.

European governments seldom attempted to prevent the emigration of their citizens, but often enough tried to dissuade them from leaving. In 1854, the Prussian government published a series of handbills about the depression threatening the United States, while Saxony issued placards pointing to the Know-Nothing campaigns.

By 1854, most of the "Forty Eighters" had decided to remain in the United States. Their money had run out, and their hopes for a German Revolution had been dashed to pieces.

The most widely publicized example of German radicalism was contained in the Louisville Platform, which was the work of such political refugees as Karl Heinzen and Bernhard Domschke. This document demanded the abolition of slavery, the enfranchisement of Negroes, and women, and a flood of social legislation. Examples such as these helped to prompt large outbursts of pre-Civil War Nativism.

In St. Nazianz, Wisconsin, Father F. Oschwald of Baden, established a Catholic Communistic society composed of 113 colonists from Baden. Because of friction with the Catholic hierarchy, he led his followers to the forests of Wisconsin, where he bought 3,000 acres of land. He and twelve elders administered the settlement.

April 6   Mass meetings of Germans assembled in Buffalo, Chicago, Louisville, Boston, Cincinnati, Galveston, and other cities to protest the repeal of the Missouri Compromise, and the opening of the public domain to slavery, as a result of the passage of the Kansas-Nebraska Act.

April 7   In Chicago, Germans marched down Michigan Avenue, to burn in effigy Stephen A. Douglas, the author of the Kansas-Nebraska Act.

May 30   The passage of the Kansas-Nebraska Act outraged large segments of German opinion, and led many German language newspapers to embrace the anti-slavery cause. Prominent "Forty Eighters" such as Friedrich Hecker, Friedrich Hassaurek, and Carl Schurz welcomed Republicanism as a suitable outlet for their idealism, and they were joined by representatives of an older German element like Gustav Körner and Friedrich Munch.

July 15   Newspapers recorded the passage of long German immigrant trains from Albany and Buffalo, heading toward the mid-west.

December   A group of Texas Germans at San Antonio, led by Adolph Douai, an old "Forty Eighter," drew up a platform which denounced slavery.

1855

By 1855, Milwaukee had become the "German Athens". This city became the distributing center for German settlers, and the focus of the beer industry in America.

The Communia colony failed, and carried Wilhelm Weitling's Arbeiterbund, and other schemes to the wall with it.

Henry Lomb, and John J. Bausch, two German immigrants who came to America in 1849, founded the famous optical company which bears their names.

Wilhelm Keil left for Oregon to found another colony, which he called Aurora. There he died in 1877.

Heinrich Steinweg, founder of the famous piano company, Steinway and Sons, came to the United States in 1850. In 1855, his piano won three prizes at the Crystal Palace Exhibition.

Virtually the whole of the German language press in the South, joined in denouncing the San Antonio Platform of the previous year.

In 1855, several Turner organizations, led by Carl Heinrich Schnauffer and Johann Straubemüller came out in favor of the German socialist movement in the United States.

By 1855, fully ninety percent of the emigration from continental Europe originated in the German states. By then, economic depression on the farms, the introduction of machinery displacing men and causing unemployment, and political persecution were the primary causes for this emigration movement.

By 1855, seventy five percent of all European cabinet makers and upholsterers in the United States were German.

The New York State Census showed that no one occupation employed more than a small fraction of New York Germans. About 15 percent were tailors, 10 percent domestic servants, but only 5 percent were laborers, waiters or carter, the rest being distributed among a great variety of occupations.

Adolph Klix established the first German coffee and chocolate factory in the United States in New York City.

June 23   Mass meetings were held by the Germans in Boston to protest or defy the enactment of liquor laws or Sunday closing laws.

July 6   Bloody encounters between Germans and nativists occurred in Louisville, Boston, and Cincinnati in the 1850's. In Columbus, Ohio, a riot broke out at a Turner picnic and shots were fired.

July 9   The Turner Hall in Cincinnati was attacked by nativists; and a large number of Germans were injured in election riots in the same year. The Germans were fierce opponents of nativism and Know-Nothingism during the years preceding the Civil War.

1856

The most unique and lasting of the German contributions to American education was the kindergarten. The first one established in the United States was organized by Mr. Carl Schurz in Watertown, Wisconsin.

Large scale and fierce Know-Nothing riots directed against German immigrants occurred in Louisville, Kentucky.

Several Mormon missions were established in the various German states, and by the time of the Civil War, several thousand German Mormons had emigrated to the United States.

By 1856, the rationalists, freethinkers and athiests among the "Forty Eighters" controlled half of the German language newspapers in the United States.

Toledo, Ohio attracted both a strong German Lutheran and a German Catholic element. They were organized into many societies. Its leading newspaper, the Toledo Express, was published by two Germans, Emil Guido, and Joseph Marx.

The Illinois-Central Railroad was largely built by Germans immigrant labor, who then settled along its route of way.

In 1856, Friedrich Kapp, a Commissioner of Emigration in New York, claimed that German immigrants were bringing with them to the United States, about $100 each.

Nearly 24,000 Germans lived in Kleindeutschland in New York City.

The San Antonio Zeitung, Adolph Douais' newspaper, lost so many customers because of its anti-slavery stand, that it went out of existence.

The desertion of the German vote to the Republican party was well under way. Leaders like Carl Schurz, Karl Hassaurek, Friedrich Froebel, Friedrich Hecker, Friedrich Munch, Gustav Körner, and Reinhold Solger spoke in many cities in behalf of the Republican ticket.

By 1856, Joseph Wedemeyer's organization was rapidly deteriorating in the East, and as a result, Wedemeyer, along with several other socialist leaders, went west. With him gone, the Marxians of the East coast lost their most effective commander.

April 7   As German immigration increased in the 1850's, so did literary clubs. A Bildungs-Verein appeared in New York in 1856, and in 1858 a Conversations Club, devoted to lectures and discussions of social and educational topics, began to operate.

June 25   It is not difficult to understand why many native Americans were alarmed by the socialism and agnosticism of the Turners, and some of the worst excesses of the nativist movement of this year was directed against the Turnerbund in New York City.

September 30   German Buchanan Clubs were organized by the Democrats and the Democratic platform was particularly forceful in its denunciation of Know-Nothingism, with which the Republicans were associated.

October   The New Yorker Staatszeitung still regarded slavery with equanimity, and C. F. W. Walther, patriarch of the German Lutherans, approved of it on biblical authority.

November 4   Many German-Americans, especially in Iowa, Ohio, and Wisconsin, supported John C. Fremont, the Republican candidate, for president. The bulk of the German voters, however, were badly divided.

1857

The Germans of Virginia held a celebration in Richmond, honoring the Revolutionary hero, Baron von Steuben. It was in part arranged to impress the nativists of the South with the strength and respectability of the German element in Virginia.

A Communist Club was created among Germans at Hoboken, New Jersey on the initiative of F. A. Sorge, Albert Komp, Fritz Jacobi, and Fr. Kamm. It was never very influential, and during the Civil War it suspended its meetings. It did, however, pioneer the formation of the International Workingmen's Association during the post-bellum period.

Hans Balatka of Munich, who later became famous in Milwaukee and Chicago as a director and composer of merit, was a member of a group of "Forty Eighters" who tried a cooperative experiment in Wisconsin in 1857.

March 6
Germans throughout the country vehemently protested the Supreme Court's decision in the Dred Scott Case, criticizing the court as pro-slavery.

1858

In 1858, as a concession to the large German element in Iowa, the prohibition law was amended to permit the manufacture and sale of beer, cider, and light wines.

The second kindergarten in America was opened by Caroline Louisa Frankenberg at Columbus, Ohio.

It took German immigrant ships as much as 96 days to reach New York from Hamburg. One ship, the Howard, reached New York with no drinking water left, a food shortage, and 37 dead from Cholera.

November
Although many Wisconsin Germans remained loyal to the Democrats, the Republicans carried Milwaukee in the Congressional elections of 1858, an event that caused nationwide comment.

1859

An incident occurred in Massachusetts which threatened to drive the Germans back into the waiting arms of the Democrats. The State Legislature there, still in the grip of the Know Nothings, attacked a clause to the Constitution, depriving all naturalized citizens of the right to vote or hold office until two years after their naturalization had been completed. Protests from Germans all over the country poured into Massachusetts, and leading Republicans, including Abraham Lincoln, were forced to reply. Germans called on their leaders to issue a formal protest, and the German press advised its readers to vote Democratic in 1860.

The German pietists at Buffalo finally moved to Iowa, where they established Amana, or the Community of the True Inspiration.

The German population of New York City was estimated at 100,000, with 20 churches, 50 schools, 10 bookstores, 5 printing establishments, and a German theater.

The Germans in New York City held an elaborate Schillerfeier, honoring the great German poet with dramatics, concerts, speeches, dances, and illuminations.

April 30   The German Fire Company of Charleston, South Caro-
               lina, entertained the visiting German Fire Company of
               Savannah, Georgia, with an elaborate banquet.

May 5   The masses of German population left educational matters
               to custom, accident, and the church.   However, the first
               Freie Deutsche Schule opened its doors in New York City.
               It was a free secular school.

May 6   Salmon P. Chase and William Seward reassured the Ger-
               mans of their opposition to all discriminations against
               the foreign-born, and German leaders like Carl Schurz
               and J. Bernhard Stallo refused to leave the Republicans.
               Apologies were made by the Republicans, and in several
               states, Germans were promptly nominated for state offi-
               ces by the Republican party.   At the Republican National
               Convention in 1860, the "Dutch Plank" was included in the
               platform to please German voters.

July 2   The New York Germans celebrated their third annual Steu-
               ben festival in a wooded grove outside the city.

November 15   Charleston Germans celebrated a Schiller anniversary with
               fireworks, a concert, and a torchlight procession.

                                    1860

               By 1860, the Turner movement was less socialistic, but
               it remained inimical to all the foes of what it termed
               progress; by 1865, the word "Socialist" was no longer
               used in the official name of the Nordamerikanischer Turn-
               ebund.

               Out of a population of nearly 38,000 in Richmond, Virginia,
               7,000 were Germans.

               The German element constituted more than thirty one per-
               cent of the total foreign-born population of the United
               States.

               The German element in Illinois exceeded 130,000, and was
               distributed through Chicago, Belleville, Galena, Quincy,
               Alton, Peoria, and Peru.

               The Census reported that 1,301,000 Germans resided in
               the United States.   Only a small number were found in
               New England, and more than one half lived in the upper
               Mississippi and Ohio Valleys, especially in the states of
               Ohio, Illinois, Wisconsin, and Missouri.

In Watertown, Wisconsin, the Germans came to hear the Milwaukee Musikverein present an opera with only piano accompaniment. It was the German immigrant, more than any other, who made the greatest contribution to the development of choral singing in nineteenth century America.

Drs. Louis and Charles Dohme founded one of the largest pharmaceutical companies in the United States in Baltimore.

Astute western politicians did not forget the importance of the German vote. Abraham Lincoln tried to master the complexities of German grammar, and prior to his nomination for the presidency, he owned a German-language newspaper for a few months.

In the campaign of 1860, in addition to Carl Schurz, Francis Lieber, H. E. Krehel, Friedrich Munch, and others made speeches for Lincoln, although their first preference was probably William H. Seward.

May 16

The extent of German influence in the Republican party was revealed at the Republican National Convention in Chicago, when the party incorporated the so-called "Dutch Planks" in its platform. These planks were drawn up at the Chicago Deutsches Haus Convention of the German Republicans, and called for homestead legislation, and for equality for native and foreign-born citizens alike.

June

Carl Schurz attempted to win the votes of German-Americans for Lincoln by going on a 21,000 mile speaking tour, which took him from the middle-west to the Pennsylvania-Dutch country.

October 6

Archbishop John Hughes and the Catholic hierarchy attacked the congregations of free and independent Catholics in New York, Richmond, and Philadelphia, who were voicing their discontent with Irish domination of the Catholic Church in America.

November 6

Recent investigations have made it clear that while many Germans voted for Abraham Lincoln in 1860, their vote was not as large nor as undividedly Republican as is usually believed. It is true, there was strong support for Lincoln in the German wards of Chicago and Cincinnati, but throughout the mid-west, substantial members of Germans especially in Wisconsin, remained faithful to Stephen A. Douglas and the Democrats. Only in Illinois, was German support solidly behind Lincoln, and proved decisive.

German Catholic areas refused to follow the lead of the "Forty Eighters" for Lincoln, and instead went overwhelmingly Democratic in the election. This was especially true in Milwaukee.

The Germans of the South had become almost completely sectionalized. In such German strongholds as New Braunfels, Texas, voting was overwhelmingly for John C. Breckenridge, the Southern Democratic candidate. Of the four candidates, only Lincoln failed to win a share of the German votes in the South. Only in Baltimore, where German artisans saw in abolition a means of eliminating the competition they suffered from slave labor, was there appreciable German sympathy for the anti-slavery movement.

GERMAN IMMIGRATION IN THE SECOND HALF OF THE NINETEENTH CENTURY - 1861-1910

1861

The German militia units in Texas were dissolved because they would not give up their Union flags.

April

Many German radicals joined the Union army when the Civil War broke out. Gustav Struve, Joseph Wedemeyer, F. Annecke, August Willich, Rudolph Rosa, and Fritz Jacobi were among this group.

In Missouri, the bulk of the Union forces consisted of German militiamen, whose loyalty may well have been decisive in thwarting secessionist attempts to take that state out of the Union.

May

General Matthew Lyon with 200 U. S. regulars and four German regiments seized control of the Confederate Camp Jackson in Missouri; and in a ten month campaign in Missouri that followed, many Germans under General Franz Sigel distinguished themselves in the battle to hold Missouri in the Union, although many also went home after their three month enlistment period had expired.

June 14

It has been estimated that 6,000 Germans in New York, 4,000 in Pennsylvania, and similar proportions elsewhere responded to Lincoln's first call for volunteers. Turner regiments such as the 9th Ohio Volunteers, and the 20th New York under Colonel Max Weber, were among the first to respond.

July 21

General Ludwig Blenker's German brigade saw action at the first Battle of Bull Run, and came out of it almost intact.

August 13

German ladies' aid societies presented flags to their departing volunteers, and German societies gave numerous concerts and entertainments to raise funds for the troops.

September 3

In New York, the National Zeitung denounced Lincoln as a dictator and abhorred his "Asiatic despotism."

1862

The flower of the American Turnebund went to the front during the Civil War, and over sixty percent of its membership took up arms in defense of the Union.

By 1862, six German pietist villages lay within a radius of six miles in the Iowa River Valley, and the village of Homestead was purchased outright to make the seventh, in order to give the community access to a railroad for its products.

As was the case in the Union Army, the Confederate forces included a number of German military companies, the most famous being the New Orleans Jägers, a brigade of German-Americans from that city.

April 6-7

At Shiloh, the Germans under Colonel August Willich fought with courage and distinction.

April 16

Texas Germans, in general, resisted the Confederate draft in a desire to remain neutral, rather than from any Union sympathies.

April 25-26

General August Büchel raised a regiment of Texas Germans from the area around New Braunfels. They participated in the unsuccessful Confederate attempt to hold the city of New Orleans against the Union advance.

May 20

German-Americans applauded the passage of the Homestead Act for which they had been agitating ever since the early 1850's.

August 29-30   At the Second Battle of Bull Run, German units under
                         Generals Schurz and Sigel fought very well.

                                        1863

                         The Buffalo Volksfreund denounced the "black Republicans"
                         and accused John C. Fremont of being a Jew from Alsace,
                         whose real name was Freiberger.

                         Because there were so many Germans within the limits
                         of the Confederacy, a Deutsches A-B-C und erstes Lese-
                         buch was published for their benefit in Richmond.

                         The Draft Law of 1863 was not popular with the Germans of
                         Milwaukee, and the Governor of Wisconsin experienced dif-
                         ficulty with the Germans over it for several months.

March 20   A German colony at Egg Harbor River in New Jersey,
                         about fifteen miles north of Atlantic City, which had been ⬥
                         organized in the 1850's, owned some 33,000 acres of land,
                         and held 3,000 settlers by 1863.

May 2-4   The Eleventh Corps, made up primarily of German troops
                         were defeated at the Battle of Chancellorsville and driven
                         back.   Generals Schurz and Adolf V. Steinwehr commanded
                         two of its three divisions.

June 27-   At Gettysburg, the German troops fought well, but again
July 4   were forced to retreat, and, as a result, came in for news-
                         paper attacks as "Cowardly Dutchmen" and "poltroons."
                         The nativist press especially, exploited this incident.

July 23   The New Yorker Staatszeitung remained loyal to the Dem-
                         ocrats, and supported Horatio Seymour for governor of
                         that state.

October 29   Many Germans were disgusted with Lincoln's conservative
                         course in the war, and a national convention of radical
                         Germans was held in Cleveland, at which fourteen states
                         were represented.   The convention advocated a radical
                         and severe program of reconstruction for the South, and
                         suggested John C. Fremont for president.

November 23-   German detachments served well in the many battles around
25   Chattannooga, particularly the 9th Ohio, and the 32nd In-
                         diana Regiments.

1864

There were draft riots among the Germans of Ozaukee and Washington Counties; Milwaukee County, Wisconsin voted for George B. McClellan in the presidential election of 1864.

May 5   General Franz Sigel was surprised and defeated at the Battle of New Market in the Shenandoah Valley. Eight other German-Americans reached the rank of Major-General in the Union Army during the Civil War; Henry W. Halleck, Carl Schurz, Godfrey Weitzel, August Willich, F. S. Salomon, F. Steinwehr, L. Stahel, and R. Kautz. In addition, there were 500 German officers of the rank of major or above including Peter J. Osterhaus, Gustav Struve, Alexander Schimmelpfennig, Hubert Dilgen, Julius Stahl, and August Moor. Ninety-six of them were killed in battle.

1865

The total number of persons born in the German states who served as volunteers in the Civil War was 176,817. These figures do not include second generation German-Americans, which raises the total to 216,000.

The number of Germans in the Confederacy has been estimated at approximately 70,000, of whom about 15,000 lived in New Orleans. One of the Louisiana regiments had six German companies and was commanded by Colonel Wilhelm Reichard. Georgia had a German artillary company commanded by Captain F. Steigen.

Only ten German private schools existed in New York City. Two of the most noted were the schools of Rösler vol Oels, founded in 1850, and that of Rudolph Dulon, opened in 1854.

October 6   The Arbeiterbund movement revived after the Civil War, when a new society called the Allegemeiner Deutsche Arbeiter-Verein was formed. It wielded considerable power in labor circles and maintained relations with the National Labor Union and the International Workingmen's Association. Many "Forty Eighters," and members of the old Communist club joined this organization.

1866

The Rappist colony at Economy, Pennsylvania reached the high water mark of its prosperity. The value of its real estate went steadily up, owing to the oil boom in Pennsylvania. After this date, the colony went into a steady decline numbering only 170 members by 1880.

An outbreak of Cholera caused hundreds of deaths among German immigrants traveling from Rotterdam to America on the National Line steamers.

With the formation of the North German Confederation, large groups of people began emigrating from Germany as a result of widespread hostility to compulsary military service brought into being by Prussian control.

January 20   The 107th Ohio Volunteers, a German regiment in the Civil War, acquired a tract of 5,000 acres in Florida, and went there in a body to raise cotton.

January 30   The most distinguished German in Louisiana was Christian Rosellius, who arrived at New Orleans in 1866. He became one of the greatest legal authorities on the Civil Code in that state.

1867

The first Socialist party in America was founded by Germans in New York City, but was very short-lived. It had developed out of the German Communist Club, and the German Workers' Society of that city.

In spite of sporadic efforts, the immigration propagand of the South after the Civil War fell far short of expectations. A few German settlements were established in Texas, Virginia, and Louisiana, but these were quite small and relatively unimportant.

1868

September   Seymour for President Clubs were formed by Germans in New York, Philadelphia, Fort Wayne and elsewhere, while Carl Schurz stumped among the Germans for Grant.

October   The Sisterdale settlement in Texas was largely a colony of German "Latin Farmers," where the classics were as evident in log cabins of these settlers as were the tools of the pioneer.

November 3   By 1868, many Germans had returned to the Democratic fold, and supported Horatio Seymour for president in preference to Ulysses S. Grant.

1869

November 6   Carl Schurz was elected to the United States Senate from Missouri.

December 28   Thd German Workingmen's Union of New York was strong enough to sponsor a course of lectures on labor organizations.

1870

After 1870, although German immigration remained large, its character changed rather markedly.   Fewer peasants and more artisans and industrial workers came to the United States in the period 1870-1890.

By 1870, the Germans in St. Louis had made distinct changes in that city's life.   The old French music, dances, and customs had capitulated before the German tide.

A national organization of the German teachers was launched with the defense of liberalism, and more concerned with the unification of Germany by any conceivable method.

March 3   Cincinnati issued a special appeal to its citizens to contribute $25,000 to entertain visiting German singers.

May 26   After the Civil War, Tennessee attracted numerous German immigrants to the neighborhood of Memphis, and 400 Swiss-Germans were induced to settle near Knoxville.

June 17   The German United Cabinet Makers had a cooperative organization which built twelve houses, managed a loan association, and owned a park for its outings.

September   The German defeat of France in the Franco-Prussian War, aroused tremendous enthusiasm among German-Americans, who held victory celebrations in all the larger American cities.

1871

The Chicago Liederkranz, directed by Hans Balatka, was founded.

The German-American press applauded Germany's great victory in the Franco-Prussian War, and hailed Otto von Bismarck's policy of unification by blood and iron.

Friedrich Kapp, a New York City Commissioner of Immigration, calculated that from 1819 to 1871, German immigration amounted to 2,358,709 and estimated that this represented an actual importation of money to the amount of half a billion dollars, and a potential productive capacity of over one and three quarter billion dollars.

July 8

A form of art founded by the Germans was that of caricature, and there were a number of German-American caricaturists of note such as Hy Mayer, C. E. Schultze, and Zim Zimmerman. But the first and greatest caricaturist in American history was Thomas Nast, who came from Landau in the Palatinate. He was most instrumental in the destruction of the Tweed Ring in New York, when he began publishing a series of devastating cartoons, in Harper's Weekly, directed against "Boss" William Marcy Tweed in 1871.

1872

In 1872, Milwaukee was the leading beer exporting center in the United States, largely as a result of the brewing and business skill of German immigrants such as Philip Best, Joseph Schlitz, Frederick Pabst, Frederick Miller, Valentin Blatz, Jacob Obermann, Franz Falk and others.

Carl Schurz and other German liberals, disgusted with radical reconstruction, the high protective tariff, and the scandals of the Grant's first administration, played a prominent part in launching the Liberal Republican revolt of this year.

A German colonization company was active in Colorado, although no mass movement of Germans to that area occurred.

May 1

Except for the German Catholics, most German-American Republicans, followed Carl Schurz into the Liberal Republican movement.

Carl Schurz presided at the Cincinnati convention of Liberal Republicans, which ended in the unfortunate choice of Horace Greeley for president.

July

A great effort was made to win the German vote for the Liberal Republicans. Schurz and other German liberal leaders addressed large German meetings, and tried to stir up enthusiasm for Greeley, which never fully materialized.

September   A mass meeting of Germans in Mobile, Alabama endorsed Horace Greeley for the presidency.

November 5   A large percentage of the German-American vote went to Greeley in the presidential election of 1872. The German-Catholics, however, split their votes between Greeley and Charles O'Conor, the candidate of the National Democratic party.

1873

The St. Louis school board established a public kindergarten, as an integral part of the public school system.

Several large groups of Russian-Germans settled in Nebraska.

The New York Oratorio Society, directed by Leopold Damrosch, gave its first concert in Knabe Hall. Its members were largely recruited from German families of the highest quality.

The second highest peak year for post-Civil War German immigration to the United States was 1873, when 149,671 Germans landed on American soil.

April 5   The Toledo Blade reported that German tutors were in great demand in well-to-do families.

April 30   The Cleveland Sängerfest was incorporated with a capital stock of $90,000.

September 1   In Columbus, Ohio, the school board had a violent altercation over the continued use of German readers, all of which were being printed in Saxony. However, the teaching of German continued until 1917.

1874

The Women's Christian Temperance Union launched a membership drive, and invaded the "Over the Rhine" saloons in Cincinnati with its preachments, until German saloon-keepers were forced to post signs reading, "No Crusaders Allowed."

Wendelin Grimm of Franconia came to the United States in 1857, and began growing Alfalfa as cattle fodder in Minnesota. No one had ever grown Alfalfa in the middle-west before this attempt. By 1874, his strain of Alfalfa was the toughest in that section of the country, and contributed greatly to American farming.

1875

George Brosius of Milwaukee, a veteran of the Civil War, was appointed Superintendent of Physical Training for the public schools of Milwaukee. He held the post until 1883, and is called the "Father Jahn" of the American Turner movement.

By 1875, there were only four German-born Congressmen in the House of Representatives.

1876

The leaders of Civil Service reform included many Germans; indeed, for a time, Carl Schurz was president of the National Civil Service Reform Association.

A National Convention of Freethinkers, including Turner and German socialists met in Philadelphia in connection with the Centennial Exposition.

June 26   General George A. Custer, and his entire command were wiped out by the Sioux Indians at the Battle of Little Big Horn. Custer was descended from a Hessian, who deserted from the British Army in 1779 by the name of H. Küster.

November 7   Germans voted for Samuel J. Tilden for President. Tilden had referred to the German Berks Country of Pennsylvania as the "Gibralter of Democracy."

1877

Carl Schurz was the first German to be appointed to a President's Cabinet, when Rutherford B. Hayes named him Secretary of the Interior.

Otto Dressel denounced German nativism as vigorously as American nativism, and declared that complete absorption of the German element was a "logical necessity." Many other German leaders did not feel the same way.

During the railroad strikes of 1877, mobs of German workers roamed the streets of Chicago, and could not be brought under control until police resorted to force, with the resulting death of several workers and policemen, and scores of injuries to both groups.

The Aurora colony of Wilhelm Keil was dissolved; its property, valued at $45,000 was divided among its members.

1878

The New Yorker Volkszeitung established and edited by Adolph Douai, became the organ of the Socialist-Labor party, and was, for years, the leading socialist newspaper in the United States.

The National Deutsch-Amerikanische Lehrerseminar was opened in Milwaukee to train teachers of German for the public schools, and to make them "true pioneers" of German culture. Its director was Max Griebach.

1879

The Bethel colony was ended; its property, valued at $65,000, was divided among its surviving members.

1880

The Census of 1880 revealed that in the cities of the United States, Germans were most prominent among the immigrant groups as tailors, carpenters, and traders.

In 1880, the official motto of the Turners was adopted; Frisch, Frei, stark, treu. Their enemies included prohibitionists and bigoted nativists among other things.

Cincinnati had twenty-five German breweries by this date.

Wisconsin continued to be attractive to German immigrants, especially because the laws of that state were hospitable to newcomers. A heavy flow of Germans began entering the state once more.

1881

The Yellowstone division of the Northern Pacific Railroad was built largely by German laborers, who then settled along its route.

George Husmann, born near Bremen, moved to California in 1881, where he became the manager of the Talcoa Vineyards in the Napa Valley. He was instrumental in saving vast grape growing interests by introducing grafts of the hearty Missouri Riverbed crossbreed grape.

Das Deutsche Theater in Cincinnati closed in 1881, when a law was passed forbidding Sunday performances. It reopened a few years later when it began to give Saturday performances.

The Boston Symphony Orchestra was founded with George Henschel, born in Breslau, as its first conductor. He was followed by Wilhelm Gericke in 1884.

September 4   In Cincinnati, when the Hecker Monument was dedicated by the Germans of that city, the parade included more than 30 different benevolent and socio-cultural organizations.

1882

Grover Cleveland spent many an evening in the German beerhalls of Buffalo, especially at Schenkelberger's where he enjoyed the sausage and the sauerkraut. He also played pinochle and 66, games particularly popular among the German element.

The highest post-Civil War year for German immigration to the United States was 1882, when 250,630 persons arrived. Thereafter, German immigration began to decline. Financial troubles, economic disarrangement, and compulsary military training accounted for this increased emigration from the Fatherland.

1883

Charles Conrad Schneider of Saxony constructed the famous cantilever bridge across the Niagara River.

The Atchison, Topeka and Sante Fe Railroad, through its foreign immigration department, extended its activities to eastern Germany, bringing over 15,000 Russian-German Mennonites to Kansas. They settled along the route of the railroad in Kansas, with branch settlements in Oklahoma and Colorado.

The former communitarian settlement of Bethel, Missouri was incorporated as a town.

Peter Paul Cahensly, a German businessman, who would later be instrumental in the formation of the St. Raphael-sverein for the protection of German immigrants, and the Katholikentagen, conferences of clergy and laity, arrived in the United States. He began to urge German parochial autonomy.

May 24   The Brooklyn Bridge, built by John and Washington Roebling, was opened for use.

July 8   In time, the German Sängerfeste became huge affairs, and involved the construction of special concert halls, and a huge budget. Buffalo built a special hall to seat 5,500 at a cost of $160,000. Seventy-eight German societies attended its opening.

November 1   The German Emigrant House of New York reported that in ten years of existence, it had furnished food and lodging to 69,989 German immigrants.

1884

Leopold Damrosch staged the first season of German opera at the Metropolitan Opera House in New York, when he gave 57 performances in the course of the winter.

The Zoar community was incorporated as an Ohio village. This was a significant step in breaking down the isolation of the settlement.

One of the last of the radical German journals in the United States, Der Arme Teufel, was founded in Detroit by Edward Muhl, and Robert Reitzel.

November 4   Most Germans supported Grover Cleveland for president, favoring his hard money policies.

1885

By 1885, the great waves of German emigration to the United States had come to an end, reflecting Germany's phenomonal progress as an industrial nation, her growing prosperity, and the extraordinary success of Otto von Bismarck's "state socialism."

The number of German teachers in the country had risen to 5,000, but already German-American leaders were complaining that the younger generation was rapidly forgetting the German tongue, and that parents no longer insisted on having their children study German in the schools.

March   The number of German born Congressmen increased to fourteen, most of them coming from German settled areas in Illinois, Missouri, Minnesota, New York, and Texas.

1886

Reverend Peter M. Abbelen, the German-born Vicar-General of the diocese of Milwaukee, complained to the Vatican on behalf of the German priests of Milwaukee, St. Louis, and Cincinnati, about the alleged hostility of Irish-born bishops to the German language and customs.

May 5   The German newspaper Arbeiter Zeitung of Chicago became the leader of the radical workingmen's press. It preached reform by violence against those in authority, and had long urged the use of dynamite to carry out this goal. Because of these sentiments, and the fact that fragments of iron picked up after the Haymarket Bomb Affair indicated that the bomb had been constructed according to the newspaper's specifications, the editors of the Arbeiter Zeitung and those associated with them, were arrested, brought to trial, condemned, and executed.

May 7   Mass meetings of Germans in Chicago and New York condemned those Germans involved in the Haymarket Affair, and affirmed their faith in the American system.

1887

A German Priests' Association was formed, and a German-American Catholic Congress was discussed, the purpose of which was to explore ways of lessening Irish dominance of the Catholic Church in America.

September 20   August Spies, publisher of the Chicago Arbeiter Zeitung, was one of those hanged in connection with the Haymarket Riot. Of the ten indicted for murder, eight were Germans.

1888

The Irving Place Theater became the home of German drama in New York City. The leading producers were Adolph Neuendorff, Henrich Conrad, Gustav Amberg, and Maurice Baumfeld.

The Russian-Germans established communities at New Danzig and Kassel, South Dakota, and Leipzig, North Dakota.

There were thirty German Catholic newspapers published in the United States by 1888.

1889

There were at least eight important German socialist dailies in the United States in 1889.

In the 1889 election in Wisconsin and Illinois, the German vote was aroused to action, when the state legislatures threatened German parocial schools. The Germans voted as a bloc defeating those candidates who had been anti-parocial schools.

1890

By 1890, 2,750,000 of the surviving immigrants in the United States were German. Nearly half of them were to found in Illinois, Michigan, Missouri, Iowa and Wisconsin.

The Census reported that more than 8,000 German farmers entered the United States, almost all going straight to the lands of the West.

The practice of using German in the public schools in those German areas in Pennsylvania was ended.

The most influential of all German churches in America, by this time, was the Missouri Synod, strictly Lutheran, sternly orthodox, emphasizing clerical authority, and insistent on reinforcing church teaching by a system of parochial schools. It had more than 1,500 churches, and 333,000 members. It especially flourished in the midwest.

Father Henrici became the leader of the Economy, Pennsylvania community.

Milwaukee possessed six daily newspapers published in the German language.

The German language press reached its peak, and had nearly 800 publications, three quarters of all the foreign newspapers in the United States. New York and Ohio had more than a hundred each, Wisconsin, Illinois, and Pennsylvania more than 80 each and Iowa and Missouri as many as 40 each.

In 1890, New York State held 499,000 Germans, Minnesota, 117,000, and Illinois, 338,000. They comprised 32, 25, and 40 percent of the total foreign born population in each state.

May 27

Whitsuntide or the German Pfingstfest was a popular German festival in late Spring. It was zealously observed by German societies, with picnics, singing, dancing, general merrymaking, and the quaffing of lager beer.

1891

Beginning in 1891 and lasting until 1892, the last great influx of Germans arrived in the United States. For this two year period, the total stood at 244,000 emigrants.

The St. Raphaelverein petitioned the Pope, complaining of the neglect of German immigrant's interests in the United States. They asked for more ethnic parishes, more German priests, seminaries in Europe to train them, and for bishops in America of German origins. This petition was known as the Lucerne Memorial and was largely the work of Peter Paul Cahensly. The Vatican refused the petition, although in practice, it tacitly accepted the national parish idea. The "Cahensylite" controversy continued into the 1900's.

1892

The great renaissance of German theater in St. Louis began with the opening of the Germania Theater. The enterprise was supported by the Germania Theater Verein whose members subscribed for a certain number of performances each year.

The last great year for German emigration to the United States was 1892, when 119,168 Germans came to American shores. Thereafter, there was an appreciable decline.

November 8

William Goebel, a German-American was elected Governor of Kentucky, and denoted that the Germans were coming of age politically.

The Germans of the mid-western states voted overwhelmingly against Populist candidates, especially James B. Weaver, the Populist nominee for President. As a group, they cast their ballots for Benjamin Harrison and the Republicans.

1893

By 1893, many German Protestants reversed their former position on nativism, and joined the American Protective Association. For these Germans, the struggle against the "new immigration" was primarily a struggle against increasing Catholicism in the United States.

At the Chicago World's Fair, 4,000 German Turners gave an exhibition of drills and gymnastics, carrying nickel-plated wands.

A National German Schützenbund (shooting club) was launched in Missouri. German sharpshooting clubs were a unique type of organization introduced by German immigrants.

November 4   John Peter Altgeld, a German-American, was elected the first Democratic Governor of Illinois. He immediately outraged public opinion by pardoning the anarchists, H. Fielden, F. Schwab, and A. Neebe, who had been convicted of the Haymarket murders in 1886. His election, however, signified that the Germans were moving up the political ladder.

1894

From 1894 onward, German immigration became almost negligible. The annual movement never exceeded 40,000, and by 1912 had fallen below 20,000.

June 23   A parade of German singers in New York City included 10,000 marchers who had come to the city to inaugurate a singing competition that lasted three days and cost $50,000.

1896

The old constitution of St. Nazianz remained in effect until 1896, when the Archbishop of Milwaukee assumed jurisdiction, and assigned the administration of the colony to one of the religious orders of the Church.

November 3   The Germans concentrated in Iowa, Kansas, Nebraska, and the Dakotas, again repudiated the Populists and voted for William McKinley and the Republicans on election day. For the most part, they opposed the free silver movement.

1897

The German Reichstag passed a law improving the conditions of emigrants leaving the German Empire, including detailed rules on space, ventilation, sanitation, and medical inspection aboard emigrant ships.

1898

The village of Zoar officially abandoned communism because of the demands of the younger generation. Each of the remaining 136 members received a cash payment, a home in the village, and some land.

May   29   German-Americans participated in all the wars of the United States. In the Spanish-American War, several men of German ancestry distinguished themselves in a number of campaigns. Admiral Winfield Schley, for example, destroyed the Spanish fleet at Santiago, Cuba.

1899

The National German-Alliance, chartered in 1899 by an Act of Congress, and dedicated to high cultural aims, became more and more absorbed in the battle against prohibition and blue laws to the neglect of other aims.

Frederick W. Halls, a German-American, was appointed Secretary of the American delegation to the First Peace Congress held at the Hague.

1900

In 1900, the Dunkard settlement at Ephrata, Pennsylvania contained only seventeen members.

Victor Berger of Milwaukee, along with Eugene V. Debs set out to "Americanize" the American Socialist party, and remove the German influences from that organization.

The German colony at Aurora, Oregon was incorporated as a town. It had a population of 122.

One third of the total population of Texas was of German blood.

The Germans ranked second in number to the Scandinavians in Minnesota.

November 6   Victor Berger was elected Mayor of Milwaukee on the
                    Socialist ticket.

                    The Germans of Wisconsin not only rallied to the Progres-
                    sive cause of Robert La Follette, whom they voted for as
                    Governor, but also, became one of the bulwarks of his
                    party.

1901

From 1901 to 1917, The Fatherland, the organ of the National German-American Alliance, was "undiluted pro-
Germanism."

1902

There were only 100 members of the St. Nazianz commune
living in cloisters, and led by five elders.

1903

In 1903, the Rappist colony at Economy, Pennsylvania had
only four members left.

1904

By 1904, the number of German-language newspapers in
the United States had dropped to 600, and this total included
78 daily newspapers.

1905

Theodore Thomas, an immigrant from Hanover, was mainly
responsible for developing a better technique for ensemble
playing, and for correct music reading.   He exerted a tremendous influence on the musical education of the American people, especially in the middle-west.

1907

The German-American Alliance, and the Ancient Order of
Hibernians came to an agreement, whereby they would joint-
ly and separately oppose all forms of immigration restric-
tion.

Only 36000 German immigrants entered the United States
out of a total immigration figure of 1,285,349.

Only 38,000 German immigrants entered the United States out of a total immigration figure of 1,285,349.

June 15

Congressman Richard Bartholdt, a German-American, was appointed President of the American delegation to the Second Hauge Peace Congress.

1908

A study revealed that 35.5 percent of all Germans who came to the United States in this year had been helped by remittances or tickets sent back to the Vaterland by Germans already in America.

1909

As late as 1909, the Bund der Freien Gemeinden und Freidenkerverein (freethinker organization) was still in existence, with seven congregations and about 1,000 members.

In 1909, the membership of the Turnerbund stood at more than 40,000 German-Americans.

1910

As of 1910, the largest single foreign born group in the United States was from Germany; it contained more than 8,200,000 persons. Most of the Germans still lived in rural areas, because during their greatest years of influx, abundant quantities of cheap and free land had been available. However, the Census reported large groups of Germans in various cities; New York, 278,000, Chicago, 182,000, Baltimore, 26,000, Milwaukee, 65,000, and Minneapolis, 9,000.

The Immigration Commission Reports indicated that 27 percent of all the Germans in the United States were still engaged in agricultural pursuits.

It was estimated that German-American farmers in the United States had developed more than 672,000 farms with a total area of 100,000,000 acres by 1910.

GERMAN IMMIGRATION IN THE TWENTIETH CENTURY
1911-1950

1911

In 1911, only 32,061 Germans emigrated to the United States.

1913

November

Resolutions of alarm drafted by some German groups with reference to the rapid assimilation of the German element in the United States were numerous before World War I, and indicated how thoroughly the German was being Americanized. The Ohio Alliance urged support of the Turnverein, German newspapers, and the German language.

1914

As late as 1914, Germans throughout the country were still holding no more than 30 percent of their religious services in English.

Frederick Weyerhauser, the German born lumber king of America died. His fortune was estimated at $300,000,000 garnered from lumber interests in the Northwest.

June 28

The German element in the United States was decidedly pro-German at the outbreak of World War I.

August 4

President Woodrow Wilson issued a proclamation of neutrality, which caused German-Americans to protest his partiality for the Allies.

September

German-American orators and newspapers defended Germany's invasion of Belgium, refuted the charge that Germany was to blame for the war, and confidently predicted her success. Simultaneously, German-American organizations undertook relief work, subscribed to the German Red Cross, and promoted the sale of German war bonds.

October

The German-American organizations conducted a vigorous campaign for an embargo on American exports of arms to the belligerents. It was widely interpreted as a German inspired attempt to overthrow neutrality.

1915

German was being taught in 135 of 275 public schools of Chicago, with an enrollment of more than 20,000 students, although protests against its being in the curriculum began to mount.

A German-American, Irish-American Alliance was formed to help keep the United States neutral in World War I.

The German-American organizations threw their full weight into an effort to stop the United States from supporting Great Britain in the war.

January

The Houston Post commented sarcastically that "Germany seems to have lost all of her foreign possessions with the exception of Milwaukee, St. Louis, and Cincinnati.

1916

The Deutsch Römisch Katholischer Zentralverein reached its greatest membership when it enrolled 150,000 in 1916.

November 7

Some German-Americans voted for Woodrow Wilson because of his anti-war stand in the campaign. Although they did not like Wilson, they were still more hostile to Theodore Roosevelt, who had been characteristically extreme in his denunciations of hyphenism. Many other Germans cast their ballots for Charles Evans Hughes, the Republican candidate, because of his platform of "straight and honest neutrality." Hughes won the support of the entire German language press, and a large number of German-American organizations.

1917

Erwin R. Bergdoll and his younger brother Grover Cleveland Bergdoll, sons of a prominent German brewing family in Philadelphia, became the nation's most publicized draft-dodgers during World War I.

The German language was removed from the curriculum of the public schools of many states when the United States entered the war.

April 6

With the United States declaration of war against Germany, complaints of the divided loyalty of the German element in America developed into widespread agitation against German-Americans. A wave of xenophobia swept the nation; excited "patriots" demanded the complete eradication of German culture. Accordingly, German music and opera were shunned, the charter of the German-American Alliance was withdrawn, towns, streets, and buildings with German names were rechristened; even sauerkraut became "liberty cabbage," while hamburgers turned into Salisbury steaks.

April

For German-Americans, the ending of neutrality was a major catastrophe, and although they suffered many petty persecutions, the mass of them accepted the decision to go to war, and gave the war effort their full support.

June

Dr. Ernst Krunwald, former conductor of the Cincinnati Symphony Orchestra, was arrested as an enemy alien.

John J. Pershing, whose great-grandfather, Frederick Pfoerschin had come to America in 1749, was appointed General-in-chief of the American Expeditionary Forces in Europe.

September

An Illinois mob lynched a German-American before he could be released from jail. He was being held because of certain "disloyal" remarks he had supposedly made.

The National German-American Alliance was voluntarily dissolved after a prolonged Congressional investigation, which proved nothing except that the organization had been pro-German before 1917, and had spent most of its energy fighting the inroads of prohibition upon personal liberty.

October

A vigilance committee in Minnesota, having forbidden a pastor to speak German, caught him praying at the bedside of a dying woman who spoke only German. They tarred and feathered him, and rode him out of town on a rail.

Bruno Walter, the conductor of the Chicago Symphony Orchestra, was suspended from his position because he had not as yet become an American citizen.

December 18

German-Americans vehemently opposed the passage of the Prohibition Amendment, which they felt violated every concept of personal liberty and tolerance.

German-Americans of the mid-west began to join the Nonpartisan League, an organization linked to progressivism in Wisconsin. They used the League as a vehicle of their resentment.

Among the more competent directors of the German plays in Cincinnati was Otto Ernst Schmid. He was in charge of Cincinnati's German Theater when World War I broke out. When three of his actors were interned as enemy aliens, the German Theater of Cincinnati closed its doors for the last time.

The wartime Mayor of Chicago, William Hale Thompson, endeared himself to the German electorate by threatening to punch the King of England in the nose, and by refusing to receive Marshall Joffre of France during his mission to the United States. The Germans of Chicago continually voted for Thompson in successive years, although his administrations were rife with corruption.

One of the first units to see action agunst Germany in World War I, was the famous 28th Division made up of National Guard units drawn from German-Americans from eastern Pennsylvania.

By the end of World War I, the number of German language newspapers in the United States had sunk to only 278 of which 26 were daily newspapers.

September

A sub-committee of the Senate's Judiciary Committee failed to establish any direct connection between the National German-Alliance and the German propaganda machine.

November 5

Middle-western Germans gave their votes to Farmer-Labor candidates in the general elections of this year. They were voicing the old Populist isolationist sentiments.

1919

An all time low of only 52 Germans emigrated to the United States.

The German-American Historical Society of Illinois declared that they were convinced of the superiority of German culture.

May

German-Americans organized the Steuben Society, which had the expressed purpose of thoroughly Amerieanizing whatever Germanism remained among the German-American element in the United States, so as to avoid a repetition of the atrocious anti-German feeling of the World War I years.

June 28

The German government signed the Treaty of Versailles. German-Americans, ignoring the fact that Germany would have been still more harshly treated but for Woodrow Wilson, blamed him for the fact that the treaty included a German war-guilt clause.

1920

There were 116,535 persons living in the United States who were born in Russia, but spoke German, and 186,997 others born in the United States of this Russian-German stock. These immigrants were essentially German and not Russian.

Germans of the mid-west and other parts of the nation adopted an isolationist viewpoint in American foreign affairs. Isolationism was not a measure of the concern German-Americans felt for the welfare of the Fatherland; it reflected, rather, the extent to which World War I had taught them to associate American involvement in war with attacks upon themselves.

August 26

German-Americans, for the most part, opposed the passage of the Woman's Suffrage Amendment which they felt smacked of puritanism and feminism.

November 2

German-Americans voted heavily for Warren G. Harding and helped to repudiate the visionary programs of the now hated Woodrow Wilson.

1921

The Amana colony had a membership of 1,500, and the value of its property was listed at more than $2,100,000.

May 19

The first Quota Law was passed, limiting German immigration to three percent of the German population in the Census of 1910. Between 1921 and 1930, only 412,202 Germans emigrated to the United States.

1922

January

Victor Berger of Milwaukee, was elected to Congress, and was finally seated after having been denied his seat by Congress in 1918 and 1919.

1923

The Supreme Court declared that all state laws prohibiting the teaching and use of German in private or parochial schools was unconstitutional.

Charles P. Steinmetz, a young German Socialist from Breslau, became one of the greatest electrical wizards in the age of electricity. Until his death in 1923, General Electric provided him with everything he asked for his work.

1924

Members were being recruited among the German communities of the United States for the National Socialist party of the United States.

May 26

The Immigration Law of 1924 cut the size of the German quota to two percent of the German population resident in the United States in 1890.

November 4

A very large segment of the German element voted for Robert M. La Follette, candidate of the Progressive Party, for the presidency.

1925

The Steuben Society became a kind of German anti-defamation league, but performed less vigorously than similar organizations formed by other ethnic groups.

German descended criminals have made their mark from time to time. Probably the most famous was the notorious Arthur Flegenheimer, alias "Dutch" Schultz, who was a highly efficient rumrunner, distributor of bootleg liquor, and gang leader in New York during prohibition.

1928

November 6

Herbert Hoover was elected President of the United States. He was the first president of German ancestry.

1929

Some of the greatest stars in baseball history were of German descent---Babe Ruth, Lou Gehrig, Honus Wagner, Rube Waddell, and Frank Frisch to mention only a few. All of the above have been inducted into baseball's Hall of Fame.

A Nazi periodical called the Vorposten was founded in Chicago promising "News of the German Movement in America."

1930

In 1930, the number of German language newspapers still published in the United States had dropped to 172.

Owing partly to the economic depression, and in part to the demands of the younger generation, Amana Colony formally abandoned Communism, and was reorganized as stock company, under the usual rules applicable to corporation in a capitalistic society.

The Missouri Synod claimed a membership of 1,163,666, with more than 3,000 pastors.

The Lancaster Sunday News and other newspapers in the "Pennsylvania Dutch" cities began to publish a series of letters and other material in the "Pennsylvania Dutch" dialect in an attempt to preserve the old language of these areas.

1932

The German-American Historical Society of Illinois Yearbook was not published after 1932.

By 1932, the attraction of the Turnerbund had declined, and national membership dropped to 27,000.

The "crime of the century," the kidnapping and murder of the baby of Charles Lindbergh Jr., was committed by Bruno Richard Hauptmann, a German immigrant.

Captain W. H. Santelmann, a native of Offensen, Germany, became the leader of the United States Marine Band.

1933

The Nazis attempted to gain control of the United German Societies of New York, which had a membership of 70,000 at this time. The move was bitterly resisted, and the organization soon broke apart.

January

The elevation of Adolf Hitler to the Chancellor's office in Germany, bitterly divided the German element in the United States on the issue of Nazism.

February 9

Twelve hundred Germans gathered at Turnhalle in New York's Yorkville section, sang Deutschland Uber Alles, the Horst Wessel Song, and heiled Hitler with Swastika-emblazoned banners.

March

The Society of the Friends of the Hitler Movement began to hold weekly meetings in various German dominated areas of the United States.

April   An organization known as the Steel Helmets was established in New York City made up of naturalized Germans
who had served in the German Army during World War I.

1934

Reverend Charles E. Coughlin of Royal Oak, Michigan
organized the National Union for Social Justice. His Sunday afternoon diatribes against the World Court, the international bankers, and the Versailles Treaty brought many
German-Americans to his support.

The court in Pennsylvania appointed a receiver for the
property of the former Dunkard settlement at Ephrata,
Pennsylvania.

A Storm Trooper Corps and a Nazi Youth Corps were established in New York City.

October   The Steuben Society strongly and forthrightly resisted the
Nazi Movement in the United States. Most German-
Americans did also.

November   The Carl Schurz Society began publishing a periodical
pointedly titled, The American-German Review. If the
hyphen had to reappear, it would be inverted.

1935

Jewish leaders in the United States withdrew their long-
standing financial and moral support of the Carl Schurz
Memorial Foundation.

The appeal of the Deutsch Römisch Katholischen Zentralverein declined, and its membership dropped to about
57,000.

1936

The principal transmitter of the Nazi doctrine in the United
States, became, in 1936, the German-American Bund. It
was actually the former New Friends of Germany in a
new guise. The New Friends held a convention in Buffalo
where they changed their name to the Deutsh-Amerikan-
ische Volksbund or German-American People's League.
It also elected a man named Fritz Lieber Kuhn as its
leader.

June   19   Father Coughlin formed the Union party, and offered
                     William Lemke as its candidate. Many mid-western Ger-
                     mans openly expressed their support of this third party
                     candidate and his platform.

November 3   Franklin Delano Roosevelt ran very well in all the German-
                     American areas of the country, as they gave him their votes
                     overwhelmingly. William Lemke polled only 890,000
                     votes. The only four cities in which he got more than five
                     percent of the vote were heavily German Catholic (St.
                     Paul, Dubuque, Boston and Cincinnati.

                                       1937

                     Forty Americans of German background, notorious for
                     their Nazi sympathies, and including G. K. Hein, Herman
                     Schwinn, and William Kunze, went to Germany for an in-
                     tensive course of indoctrination, and to attend the Fifth
                     Congress of Germans Abroad in Stuttgart.

                     The American Nazi Party had 200,000 members by 1937.
                     Seventy-eight different units had been organized, the lar-
                     gest in New York City, Los Angeles, San Francisco, Seat-
                     tle, Detroit, Toledo, Cleveland, Pittsburgh, Boston, Balti-
                     more, Buffalo, Newark, Schenectady, Sheboygan, and
                     Washington, D. C.

                     The long settled Germans in St. Louis and Milwaukee,
                     turned their backs on the German-American Bund, and
                     without the support of those millions, the Bund did not
                     have a chance except as a lunatic fringe movement.

                                       1938

                     Of the German population in the United States in 1938, 70
                     percent were totally indifferent to the appeal of internation-
                     al Nazism, 20 percent were definitely anti-Nazi, 9 percent
                     were pro Nazi, and 1 percent were rabidly, militantly Nazi.

                     In Milwaukee, the Bund had on its rolls only a few hundred
                     families, and in Wisconsin, in general, it simply dried up
                     completely in a few months.

                                       1939

February 20   Perhaps the most sensational display of Nazi influence came
                     at New York's Madison Square Garden, when 22,000 mem-

bers of the German-American Bund held a rally, replete with armbands, swastikas, and storm troopers. Actually many who came were anti-Nazi, and brawls broke out between the mock storm troopers and spectators, who could not restrain their amusement at some of the cruder remarks from the platform. Police had to intervene to quell the disturbances.

April   The German-American Bund came under attack by Congress, which passed a resolution of Representative Martin Dies of Texas, calling for an investigation of all un-American activities.

May   The German-American establishment began attacking the activities of Fritz Kuhn and the Bund.

September 1   German-American attachment to isolationism became even stronger after World War II broke out.

November   Fritz Kuhn was convicted in a New York Court of misappropriating his organizations' funds, and was sent to prison.

1940

Between 1931 and 1940, 114,058 Germans entered the United States. Most of those who came, had emigrated to escape Nazi tyranny.

November 5   Franklin D. Roosevelt's share of the German-American vote dropped by almost 35 percent. The suspicion that F. D. R. was heading toward another intervention in Europe caused great resentment among the German communities in the United States.

1941

December 8   When World War II was declared on Germany, the mass of German-Americans exhibited little sympathy with the aspirations, even less with the methods of Adolph Hitler and the Nazis. For the most part, hyphenated Americanism was a dead issue.

1942

General Dwight D. Eisenhower, a descendent of German settlers in Texas, was appointed commander of United States forces in the European theater of war. Other notable Americans of German ancestry who fought in World

War II were Admiral Chester Nimitz, General Carl Spaatz, and many others.

1946

According to a report compiled by the United States Attorney General, a German-American, George Sylvester Viereck, had acted as a confidential agent for the German Propaganda Ministry in the United States. He had received $350,000 from the Nazi Government for propaganda purposes.

1950

Between 1941 and 1950, 226,578 Germans entered the United States. Many came after World War II was over under the Displaced Persons Act.

By 1950, only 61 German newspapers were being published in the United States, and most of those were local, religious and trade publications, partly printed in English.

THE HYPHENATED GERMAN IS GONE, 1951-1970

Even before 1951, the visible and physical Germanic influences upon American life and culture had all but disappeared or had been homogenized. To be sure, Germans continued to emigrate to the United States during this twenty year period, but the assimilation process for these newcomers was rapid and hardly discussible. With the exception of the years 1951, 1952 and 1957, when 87,755, 104,236, and 60,353 Germans respectively came to the United States, German emigration did not exceed 33,000 in any other single year. In 1969 and 1970, for example, German emigration to the United States was 9,289 and 9,684. Moreover, American culture, in the process of absorption, has left only the faintest individual immigrant stamp during these last two decades.

DOCUMENTS

The documents section of this book is designed to act as a starting point for those students interested in pursuing the subject of German immigration further. The documents selected here, are only a fraction of the huge mass of primary materials available for research. They were chosen, however, to give the reader a broad variety of the different aspects of the German-American experience. In addition to the documents contained herein, there are literally scores of other government papers, diaries, letters, state and local records, and contemporary accounts dealing with the subject. To be sure, no central repository of these materials exists, and the researcher will have to search out the materials for himself from a variety of places scattered across the country. Moreover, while most of the primary works have been translated, a reading knowledge of German can prove most helpful, especially when dealing with the hundreds of surviving editions of the various German-language newspapers.

Obviously much more could have been included in this document section, but space limitations prevented the author from doing so. Space limitations, aside, the documents that follow cover most time periods of German immigration to and in the United States, and were culled from a number of different sources. Finally, the author has deliberately avoided including primary materials concerned with German-Jews in America, for although this group constituted an important, if small part of the German movement, they fall more appropriately into the Jewish immigrant experience in America.

THE GERMANS IN PENNSYLVANIA-1684

In 1683, Francis Daniel Pastorius, a German lawyer, led a group of Mennonites to Pennsylvania. There, they laid out the town of Germantown, which became a model for similar settlements. (Source: Francis D. Pastorius, "Description of Pennsylvania, 1700," Old South Leaflets, vol. IV, No. 95, pp. 4-6, 7-8, 12-16.)

The German Society commissioned myself, Francis Daniel Pastorius, as their licensed agent, to go to Pennsylvania and to superintend the purchase and survey of their lands. I set out from Frankfurt . . . , went to London, where I made the purchase, and then embarked for America. Under the protection of the Almighty, I arrived safely at Philadelphia, and I was enabled to send my report home to Germany on the 7th of March, 1684. . . .

Our first lot in the city is of the following dimensions. It has one hundred feet front, and is four hundred feet deep. Next to it is to be a street; adjoining it lies the second lot of the same size . . . . . Then another street. Lot No. 3 joins this street, its size being the same as the other two. On these lots, we can build two dwellings at each end, making in all, twelve buildings with proper yards and gardens, and all of them fronting on the streets.

For the first few years, little or no profit can reasonably be expected to accrue from these lots, on account of the great scarcity of money in this province, and also, that as yet this country has no goods or productions of any kind to trade with or export to Europe.

Our Governor, William Penn, intends to establish and encourage the growing and manufactory of woolens; to introduce the cultivation of the vine, for which this country is peculiarly adapted, so that our Company had better send us a quantity of wine-barrels and vats of various sorts, also all kinds of farming and gardening implements. Item, an iron stove, several blankets and mattresses, also a few pieces of Barchet and white linens, which might be sold in our trading-house here, to good advantage . . . . .

Another English Company have laid out the new town of Frankfort, five miles above Philadelphia, at which, now so flourishing and pleasant place, they have already established several good mills, a glass-house, pottery, and some stores and trading-houses. New Castle lies forty miles from the ocean, on the Dellavarra, and has a very good harbor. The town of Uplandt is twenty miles above New Castle, on the river, and is a fine large place inhabited mostly by Swedes.

On the twenty-fourth day of October 1685, have I, Francis Daniel Pastorius, with the wish and concurrence of our Governor, laid out and planned a new town, which we called Germantown or Germanopolis, in a very fine and fertile district, with plenty of springs of fresh water, being well supplied with oak, walnut and chestnut trees, and having besides excellent and abundant pasturage for the cattle. At the commencement, there were but twelve families of forty-one individuals, consisting mostly of German mechanics and weavers. The principal street of this, our town. I made sixty feet in width, and the cross street forty feet. The space or lot for each house and garden, I made three acres in size; for my own dwelling, however, six acres.

Before my laying out of this town, I had already erected a small house in Philadelphia, thirty feet by fifteen in size. The windows, for the want of glass, were made of oiled paper . . . .

I have also obtained fifteen thousand acres of land for our Company, in one tract, with this condition. ---that within one year at least thirty families should settle on it; and thus we may, by God's blessing, have a separate German province, where we can all live together in one . . . .

We Christians acknowledge as our Governor and chief magistrate the oft-named and excellent, the Honorable William Penn, to whom this region was granted and given as his own, by His Majesty of England, Charles II, with the express command that all the previous and future colonists should be subject to Penn's laws and jurisdiction.

This wise and truly pious ruler and governor did not, however, take possession of the province thus granted without having first conciliated, and at various councils and treaties duly purchased from the natives of this country the various regions of Pennsylvania. He, having by these means obtained good titles to the province, under the sanction and signature of the native chiefs, I therefore have purchased from him some thirty thousand acres for my German-colony.

Now, although the oft-mentioned William Penn is one of the sect of Friends or Quakers, still he will compel no man to belong to his particular society, but he has granted to every one free and untrammeled exercise of their opinions, and the largest and most complete liberty of conscience . . . .

Our German society have in this place now established a lucrative trade in woolen and linen goods, together with a large assortment of other useful and necessary articles, and have entrusted this extensive business to my own direction; besides this they have now purchased and hold over thirty thousand acres of land, for the sake of establishing an entirely German colony. In my newly laid out Germantown, there are already sixty-four families in a very prosperous condition. Such persons, therefore, and all those who still arrive, have to fall to work and swing the axe most vigorously, for wherever you turn the cry is Itur in antiquam sylvam, nothing but endless forests; so that I have been often wishing for a number of Stalwart Tyrolians, to throw down these gigantic oak and other forest trees, but which we will be obliged to cut down ourselves by degrees, and with almost incredible labor and exertion; during which we can have a very forcible illustration of the sentence pronounced upon our poor old father Adam, that in the sweat of his brow he should eat his bread. To our successors, and others coming after us, we would say, that they must not only bring over money, but a firm determination to labor and make themselves useful to our infant colony. Upon the whole, we may consider that man blessed whom the devil does not find idling . . . .

A GERMAN SETTLEMENT IN THE VIRGINIA UPCOUNTRY-1715

Most German settlers were poor, and in Virginia, they constituted a weak shield against the Indians. This selection, written
by John Fontaine, a Huguenot, described a German settlement
in Virginia's upcountry in November, 1715.
(Source: Ann Maury, Memoirs of a Huguenot Family (New York,
1853.)

We continued on our way until we came five miles above this land, and
there we went to see the Falls of Rappahannoc River. The water runs with
such violence over the rocks and large stones that are in the river, that it is
almost impossible for boat or canoe to go up or down in safety. After we
had satisfied our curiosity, we continued on the road. About five we
crossed a bridge that was made by the Germans, and about six we arrived
at the German settlement. We went immediately to the minister's house.
We found nothing to eat, but lived on our small provisions, and lay upon
good straw. We passed the night very indifferently.

21st Our beds not being very easy, as soon as it was day, we got up.
It rained hard, but notwithstanding, we walked about the town, which is
palisaded with stakes stuck in the ground, and laid close the one to the
other, and of substance to bear out a musket-shot. There are but nine
families, and they have nine houses, built all in a line; and before every
house, about twenty feet distant from it, they have small sheds built for
their hogs and hens, so that the hog-sties and houses make a street. The
place that is paled in is a pentagon, very regularly laid out; and in the very
centre there is a blockhouse, made with five sides, which answer to the
five sides of the great inclosure; there are loop-holes through it, from
which you may see all the inside of the inclosure. This was intended
for a retreat for the people, in case they were not able to defend the pali-
sadoes, if attacked by the Indians.

They make use of this block-house for divine service. They go to
prayers constantly once a day, and have two sermons on Sunday. We
went to hear them perform their service, which was done in their own
language, which we did not understand; but they seemed to be very devout,
and sang the psalms very well.

This town or settlement lies upon Rappahannoc River, thirty miles
above the Falls, and thirty miles from any inhabitants. The Germans
live very miserable. We would tarry here some time, but for want of
provisions we are obliged to go. We got from the minister a bit of smoked
beef and cabbage, which were very ordinary and dirtily drest.

We made a collection between us three of about thirty shillings for
the minister, and about twelve of the clock we took our leave, and set out
to return; the weather hazy, and small rain.

THE PALATINE GERMANS IN NEW YORK-1720

In 1720, a group of Palatine Germans who had been settled in upper New York State by the British government, petitioned the King for aid, detailing their grievances and mistreatment at the hands of British officials in the colony of New York.
(Source: Edmund Bailey O'Callaghan, ed., Documents Relative To The Colonial History of New York (Albany, 1855.)

That, In the year 1709. The Palatines, & other Germans, being invited to come into England about Four Thousand of them were sent into New York in America, of whom about 1700 Died on Board, or at their landing in that Province, by unavoidable sickness.

That before they went on Board, they were promised, those remaining alive should have forty acres of Land, & Five pounds sterling per Head, besides Cloths, Tools, Utensils & other necessaries, to Husbandry to be given at their arrival in America.

That on their landing their they were quartered in Tents, & divided into six companies, having each a captain of their own Nation, with a promise of an allowance of fifteen Pounds per annum to each commander.

That afterwards they were removed on Lands belonging to Mr. Livingstone, where they erected small Houses for shelter during the winter season.

That in the Spring following they were ordered into the woods, to make Pitch & Tar, where they lived about two years; But the country not being fit to raise any considerable quantity of Naval Stores, They were commanded to Build, to clear & improve the ground, belonging to a private person.

That the Indians having yielded to Her late Majesty of pious memory a small Tract of Land called Schorie for the use of the Palatines, they in fifteen days cleared a way of fifteen miles through the woods & settled fifty Families therein.

That in the following Spring the remainder of the said Palatines joined the said fifty families so settled therein Schorie.

But that country being too small for their encreasing families, they were constrained to purchase some Neighbouring Land of the Indians for which they were to give Three hundred pieces of Eight.

And having built small Houses, & Hutts there about one year after the said purchase some gentlemen of Albani, declared to the Palatines, that themselves having purchased the said countrie of Schorie of the Governor of New York they would not permit them to live there, unless an agreement were also made with those of Albany; But that the Palatines having refused to enter into such an agreement, A Sheriff & some officers were sent from Albany to seize one of their Captains, who being upon his Guard; The Indians were animated against the Palatines; but these found means to appease the Savages by giving them what they would of their own substance.

That in the year 1717 the Governour of New York having summoned the Palatines to appear at Albani, some of them being deputed went thither accordingly, where they were told, that unless they did agree with the Gentlemen of Albany, the Governor expected an order from England to transport them to another place, And that he would send twelve men to view their works & improvements to appraise the same & then to give them the value thereof in money.

But this not being done the Palatines to the number of about three Thousand, have continued to manure & to sew the Land that they might not be starved for want of Corn & food.

For which manuring the Gentlemen of Albani have put in prison one man and one woman, & will not release them, unless they have sufficient security of One Hundred Crowns for the former.

Now in order that the Palatines may be preserved in the said Land of Schorie, which they have purchased of the Indians, or that they may be so settled in an adjoining Tract of Land, as to raise a necessary subsistance for themselves & their families, they have sent into England Three Persons one of whom is since dead humbly to lay their Case before His Majesty, not doubting but that in consideration of the Hardships they have suffered for want of a secure settlement, His Majestys Ministers and Council will compassionate those His faithful Subjects;

Who, in the first year after their arrival willingly and cheerfully sent Three Hundred men to the expedition against Canada, & afterwards to the Assistance of Albani which was threatened by the French and Indians, for which service they have never received One Penny tho' they were upon the Establishment of New York or New Jersey nor had they received one Penny of the five pounds per head promised at their going on board from England Neither have their commanders received anything of the allowance of fifteen pounds per Annum, and tho' the arms they had given them at the Canada expedition which were by special order from Her late Majesty, to be left in their possession, have been taken from them, yet they are still ready to fight against all the enemies of His Majesty & those countrys whenever there shall be occasion to shew their hearty endeavors for the prosperity of their generous Benefactors in England as well as in America.

Therefore they hope from the Justice of the Right Honble the Lords Commissioners of Trade and Plantations, to whom their Petition to their Excellencies the Lords Justices has been referred That they shall be so supported by their Lordships Report, as to be represented fit objects to be secured in the Land they now do inhabit or in some near adjoining lands remaining in the right of the Crown in the said Province of New York.

PROMOTING GERMAN EMIGRATION–1750

This selection, a letter from a German Lutheran pastor, describes the techniques used to promote emigration to America from the various German states.
(Source: Letter From Peter Brunnholtz, May 21, 1750, found in Reports of the United German Evangelical Lutheran Congregations in North America (Hallesche Nachrichten Series No. 2), pp. 412-14.)

Last autumn about twenty-five ships arrived here with Germans. The number of those who arrived alive was 1,049, among whom there were also about twelve who were in part regular schoolmasters in the old country, but on account of small pay, and in the hope of improvement, moved into this, and in part they had been engaged in other pursuits. They would have better remained where they were. Some come who in part have public certificates, and in part letters to me from their parsons. I, however, can help them but little. In this month, ships again frequently arrive with Germans, so that about ten have already come. The province is crowded full of people, and living becomes continually more expensive. Those who come in free--who had something in the old country, but consumed that which they had on an expensive voyage---and see that it is otherwise than was represented to them, whine and cry. Woe on the emigrants, who induced them to this! One of these in Germantown had wished to shoot himself recently from desperation. The Newlanders, as they are here called, are such as do not work, and still wish to become rich speedily, and for this reason they go out into Wurttemberg and vicinity, and persuade the people to come into this country, alleging that everything was here that they could wish for, that such a country like this there was none in the world, and that everyone could become as rich as a nobleman, etc. These deceivers have this profit in it, that they with their merchandise are brought in free, and in addition, for every head they bring to Amsterdam or to Rotterdam, they receive a certain sum from the merchants. The owners of these vessels derive much money herefrom in freightage. They pack them into the ships as if they were herring, and when they arrive, there are so many sick and dying among them that it is pitiful to behold them. Those, however, who have nothing, and are in debt also for their passage, are taken into small huts, where they lie upon straw, and are corrupted like cattle, and in part half deprived of their reason, so that they can scarcely perceive anything of the parson's consolations. The government and assembly have meanwhile made some ordinances and institutions, but whether the difficulty will be remedied thereby time will show. It would be just and right if a regular report of such things were put into the German newspapers here and there in Europe. Still what good would it do? The farmers don't get to read the papers, and many indeed would not believe it, as they moreover have a mind to come.

Gottlieb Mittleberger came to the colonies in 1750, and after a
four year stay returned home to counter rosy accounts of America,
with his own report on the miseries induced by German-speaking
immigrants, especially the "redemptioners." This selection is a
portion of that report.
(Source: Gottlieb Mittleberger, Journey to Pennsylvania in the
Year 1750 and Return to Germany in the Year 1754 (Translated
by Carl T. Eben, New York, 1898.)

This journey lasts from the beginning of May to the end of October,
fully half a year, amid such hardships as no one is able to describe ade-
quately with their misery.

The cause is because the Rhine-boats from Heilbronn to Holland
have to pass by 36 custom-houses, at all of which the ships are examined,
which is done when it suits the convenience of the custom-house officials.
In the meantime the ships with the people are detained long, so that the
passengers have to spend much money. The trip down the Rhine alone lasts
therefore 4, 5, and even 6 weeks.

When the ships with the people come to Holland, they are detained
there likewise 5 or 6 weeks. . . . .

Both in Rotterdam and in Amsterdam the people are packed densely,
like herrings so to say, in the large sea-vessels. One person receives
a place of scarcely 2 feet width and 6 feet length in the bedstead, while many
a ship carries four to six hundred souls; not to mention the innumerable implements, tools, provisions, water-barrels and other things which likewise
occupy much space.

On account of contrary winds it takes the ships sometimes 2, 3, and 4
weeks to make the trip from Holland to Kaupp (Cowes) in England. But
when the wind is good, they get there in 8 days or even sooner . . . . .
Many suffer want already on the water between Holland and Old England.

When the ships have for the last time weighed their anchors near the
city of Kaupp (Cowes) in Old England, the real misery begins with the long
voyage. For from there the ships, unless they have good wind, must often
sail 8, 9, 10 to 12 weeks before they reach Philadelphia. But even with
the best wind the voyage lasts 7 weeks.

But during the voyage there is on board these ships terrible misery,
stench, fumes, horror, vomiting, many kinds of seasickness, fever, dysen-
tery, headache, heat, constipation, boils, scurvy, cancer, mouth-rot, and the
like, all of which come from old and sharply salted food and meat, also from
very bad and foul water, so that many die miserably.

Add to this want of provisions, hunger, thirst, frost, heat, dampness,
anxiety, want, afflictions and lamentations, together with other trouble, as
c. v. the lice abound so frightfully, especially on sick people, that they can
be scraped off the body. The misery reaches the climax when a gale rages
for 2 or 3 nights and days, so that everyone believes that the ship will go to
the bottom with all human beings on board. In such a visitation the people
cry and pray most piteously. . . .

At length, when, after a long and tedious voyage, the ships come in sight of land, so that the promontories can be seen, which the people were so eager and anxious to see, all creep from below on deck to see the land from afar, and they weep for joy, and pray and sing, thanking and praising God. The sight of the land makes the people on board the ship especially the sick and the half dead, well again so that their hearts leap within them, they shout and rejoice, and are content to bear their misery in patience, in the hope that they may soon reach the land in safety. But alas!

When the ships have landed at Philadelphia after their long voyage, no one is permitted to leave them except those who pay for their passage or can give good security; the others, who cannot pay, must remain on board the ships till they are purchased, and are released from the ships by their purchasers. . . .

The sale of human beings in the market on board the ship is carried on thus: Every day Englishmen, Dutchmen and High-German people come from the city of Philadelphia and other places, in part from a great distance, say twenty, thirty, or forty hours away, and go on board the newly arrived ship that has brought and offers for sale passengers from Europe, and select among the healthy persons such as they deem suitable for their business, and bargain with them how long they will serve for their passage-money, which most of them are still in debt for. When they have come to an agreement, it happens that adult persons bind themselves in writing to serve three, four, five, or six years for the amount due by them, according to their age and strength. But very young people, from 10 to 15 years, must serve till they are 21 years old.

When people arrive who cannot make themselves free, but have children under five years, the parents cannot free themselves by them; for such children must be given to somebody without compensation to be brought up, and they must serve out their bringing up till they are 21 years old. Children from five to ten years, who pay half price for their passage, viz., thirty florins, must likewise serve for it till they are twenty-one years of age; they cannot, therefore, redeem their parents by taking the debt of the latter upon themselves. But children above ten years can take part of their parents' debt upon themselves.

A woman must stand for her husband if he arrives sick, and in like manner a man for his sick wife, and take the debt upon herself or himself, and thus serve five or six years not alone for his or her own debt, but also for that of the sick husband or wife. But if both are sick, such persons are sent from the ship to the sick-house [hospital] , but not until it appears probable that they will find no purchasers. As soon as they are well again they must serve for their passage, or pay if they have means.

When a husband or wife has died at sea, when the ship has made more than half of her trip, the survivor must pay or serve not only for himself or herself, but also for the deceased.

When both parents have died over half-way at sea, their children, especially when they are young and have nothing to pawn or to pay, must stand for their own and their parents' passage, and serve till they are 21 years old. When one has served his or her term, he or she is entitled to a new suit of clothes at parting; and if it has been so stipulated, a man gets in addition a horse, a woman, a cow. . . .

This selection is an account of the journey of Bishop John Frederick Reichel of the Moravian Church to a German frontier outpost in North Carolina. The Bishop had been sent from Germany to inspect the Moravian communities in America, and to make sure they were organized in accordance with the rules of the church. (Source: Reise-Diarium der Geschew. Reichels, 1780.)

May 22, 1780. Journeying from Lititz in Pennsylvania to Salem in the Wachau (North Carolina), we reached Anderson's Ferry, where the Susquehannah is one and one-quarter miles wide. On the side from which we approached there is a high sandy bank, and the wheels of Conrad's wagon sank to the axle in the sand, and were freed only after one and a half hours of work with levers and extra horses. On the other side is a high stony ridge. We were so fortunate as to get our two wagons and three riding horses across within two hours, by means of two Flats, which are too small for a river of such considerable size; but frequently travelers are detained here for an entire day. Each crossing takes only ten minutes, and the ferrymen race with each other. But they had to cross over and back three times, and the loading and unloading takes as much time as the crossing. Here they charge $56 (Continental) for taking over a six-horse wagon, and $8 for a horse and rider; at Wright's Ferry, where the Susquehannah is two miles wide, the charge is $90 for a six-horse wagon, and $12 for a horse and rider. Some two miles from the Susquehannah, on a creek called Susquehannah Creek, we made our first outdoor night camp, in a pretty open space surrounded by tall trees.

The 23. After strengthening ourselves with coffee at breakfast we traveled to the top of the Susquehannah ridge, from whence a beautiful view of plantations, houses, fields, orchards and meadows, hills and valleys, extended all the way to York, which we reached about eleven o'clock. We made 17 miles today, and camped for the night on a green hill close by a house. Here for the first time we were all in tents, and rested very well.

The 24. It was so cold a morning that we could scarcely keep warm at breakfast. We broke camp at six o'clock. This morning in a rough piece of woodland, Conrad's wagon, in going down a hill, ran into a tree and crushed the left front wheel. We thanked the Saviour that the wagon and horses were not thrown to the ground, for it looked as if that might easily have happened. This accident detained us an hour until the wagon could be repaired. At one-thirty we reached Hanover where we had a beautiful midday rest in a barn. We refreshed ourselves on the good beer to be obtained here. Toward evening we passed through Petersburg and camped for the night two miles farther on, on the Maryland line.

The 25. The morning again was cool. It was after six o'clock when we broke camp. Taneytown is a little village with one solitary street, lying seven miles from our camp at a point where the forests are sprinkled with pines. The road thither was full of people today, as it was the Catholic festival of Corpus Christi and they were going to the Catholic Church in

Taneytown. On the way we passed the home of Adam Loesch, and spoke with him. He was planning to sell his house and move to Holston River in Virginia, four hundred miles from there. Beyond Taneytown, which we had reached at nine-thirty, Hauser's wagon almost upset. Br. Reichel had alighted when to our pleasure we were met by Br. Schweisshaupt, and the two Brethren Weller and Kaimpf from Monocacy, the road from the latter place here coming out into the main road to Frederick, Maryland. They showed us the way to a pretty midday resting place on Pine Creek, over which there is a bridge now impassable.

Br. Schweisshaupt and the two Brn. from Monocacy, who were able to supply us with fresh provision, accompanied us for two miles to the place where the road from Baltimore to Monocacy crosses the road to Carolina at right angles, then took friendly leave of us, commending us to the good guidance of our God. From there it is nine miles to Monocacy, and about fifty to Baltimore. Today we made twenty miles, and camped about seventy-five to Baltimore. Today we made twenty miles, and camped about seventy-five miles from Lititz and eight from Frederick, in a beautiful green spot . . . .

The 14. In the morning we came to within a short mile of the Mayo River. As we rested by a beautiful spring we were joined by a Presbyterian minister, who came hither from Virginia last spring, and who asked us all sorts of questions concerning our position on political matters, and after an earnest but discreet conversation bade us a friendly farewell. There is an outdoor pulpit here where he probably preaches. The semblance of a pulpit is built of logs and boards fastened between two trees; the benches are of logs, resting on blocks.

The 15. We rose early and took up our journey with joy, crossing the Dan River safely, and reaching the Brethren in Salem at about six in the evening, thankful to the Saviour who had guided and led us like children, and had given us to feel His peace and presence throughout the entire way. We were welcomed with trombones, which played "Euren Eingang segen Gott."

June 16. The wagons, which were left behind yesterday, arrived safely this morning. And so we are in Salem, in this town of the Lord's peace-may He bless us and be with us in all we shall do for Him. Amen.

During the eighteenth century, German immigrants began settling in Baltimore and its environs. By 1800, they constituted a sizeable percentage of the city's population. In this selection, an anonymous author described life among the Germans in this thriving seaport.

(Source: [Anon] , Reise von Hamburg nach Philadelphia, Hamburg, Germany, 10.)

. . . . The German in America is not a great favorite; superior women are not well-disposed toward him. In Baltimore, however, this situation is not so prevalent. Here the number of Germans is large. But newcomers discover that their countrymen in America are not what they were in the Fatherland. American manners of thinking often influence their conduct. They try to ape the Americans, and lose their sense of discipline. Perhaps the attempt to be like the Americans, nowhere so prominent as in Baltimore, accounts for the friendliness of the maidens to the Germans. Many young German merchants have married into well-connected families and thereby cut their last ties with the homeland. Alas, there are also some fine young men who came to Baltimore innocent in heart and were duped by attractive women. These men must pay dearly for their errors, losing peace and good name. A substantial young man fell into the clutches of one of these worthless females who emptied his pockets and led him into the most shameful dealings. Having already abandoned several men, she wished to complete her ruinous work by marrying him and he was too much enraptured with her to deny her anything. But his countrymen took a hand in the matter. Although he had, out of shame, avoided them and not confided in them they felt obliged to rescue him. Against his will, they took him to a ship, sails set, which brought him back to his homeland.

The German women who marry in Baltimore do not live in the pleasantest circumstances. There are only a few here, and these are, on the whole, obliged to stay by themselves. The American women do not seek their company and let them know, in no uncertain terms, that they are reluctant to become acquainted. One of these Germans is a very clever person and contrives to keep herself well-occupied. She seems capable of circumventing very easily the whims of the Americans. I only wish that fate had blessed this good women with a more suitable man than her husband. Money alone does not always lead to happiness, nor travel to understanding. This man, who has enjoyed both advantages, still does not know how to provide for the happiness of himself or his family . . . .

German immigrant passengers were very often subjected to bad treatment by greedy ship captains and owners. Andreas Geyer Jr., a German immigrant himself, wrote about this ruthless exploitation in 1805.

(Source: Andreas Geyer Jr., "Letter to the German Society of Philadelphia," found in Friedrich Kapp, Immigration and the Commissioners of Immigration (New York, 1870.)

I went to visit those unfortunate people, and in truth they may be called unfortunate. And I must confess I have seen a number of vessels at Philadelphia with redemptioners, but never did I see such a set of miserable beings in my life. Death, to make use of the expression, appeared to be staring them in the face. The complaints were numerous which they made against the captain respecting the bad treatment they received from him on and during the passage . . . .

They left Hamburg some time in November last, and arrived at Tonningen, where lay the ship General Wayne, John Conklin, Master, bound for New York, with whom they entered into a certain agreement, on the condition that he, the said Conklin, would take them to New York, that during the passage they should be allowed a certain quantity of bread, meat, peas, fish, vinegar, butter, potatoes, tobacco, etc., as also a dram in the morning, as will appear by a reference to the agreement itself, each passenger having one.

About fourteen days after they left Tonningen they put into an English port near Portsmouth, where they remained about four weeks. . . . During that time a British recruiting officer came on board the ship, when the captain informed them that they now had an opportunity of enlisting, that those who so chose to do might, as the recruiting officer was on board the ship. Ten men consented, and entered their names, giving to the other passengers their reasons for so doing, namely, that, having been already put on allowance by the captain, they were apprehensive that, should they stay on board the ship, they should be starved before they arrived in America. Amongst those that enlisted was a man who had a wife and child on board the ship. . . Eight days after they had thus entered their names they were taken from the ship by the recruiting officer, although some of them wished to withdraw their names, but to no effect; go they must. The woman and her child are now at Amboy, lamenting the loss of the husband and father.

On the last day of their remaining in this British port, the same recruiting officer came the third time on board the ship, when the mate called four or five of the passengers by name, and told them, in the presence of the captain, they must be soldiers and go with the officer. They replied they had no intention of being soldiers, they wished to go to America. Whereupon the captain and mate seized one of them by name Samuel Vogel, and threw him into the boat belonging to the recruiting officer, which was alongisde of the ship. However, Vogel got back again into the ship, went below, and hid himself, but was again compelled to come forward with his clothes, when the recruiting officer, observing him weep, declared he would not have him, and left the ship, mentioning that he should not have come on board had not the captain, the day before, pressed him so to do. The captain was highly dissatisfied with these men for refusing to go, and declared that they should not have anything to eat on board the ship, that they might starve, and ordered one of them to be flogged for refusing, which was performed, too, in a cruel manner.

. . . .The whole of the passengers, when at this British port, complained to the captain that the treatment they received was not such as was agreed to between them at Tonningen. He replied they were not then in Tonningen, neither were they in America, but in England.

They then set sail, and after fourteen days had elapsed the captain informed them that they would get nothing to eat except bread and meat. After this each person received two biscuits, one pint of water, and the eighth part of a pound of meat per day. This regulation continued for two or three weeks, when they one and all declared they could not any longer exist on the small allowance they received; that they must, without doubt, perish. The hunger and thirst being at this time so great, and the children continually crying out for bread and drink, some of the men, resolved, at all events to procure bread, broke open the apartment wherein it was kept, and took some. This was discovered by the captain, as were also those who did the same, when each of them was ordered to, and actually did, receive, after being first tied, a number of lashes on their bare backs well laid on. The whole of the passengers were also punished for this offence. The men received no bread, the women but one biscuit.

This continued for nine days, when the men were again allowed one biscuit per day; however, the captain would at least make or proclaim a fast day. In this situation their condition became dreadful, so much so that five and twenty men, women and children actually perished for the want of the common necessities of life, in short, for the want of bread. The latter were ten in number, all at the time at the breasts of their mothers. The hunger was so great on board that all the bones about the ship were hunted up by them, pounded with a hammer and eaten; and what is more lamentable, some of deceased persons, not many hours before their death, crawled on their hands and feet to the captain, and begged him, for God's sake, to give them a mouthful of bread or a drop of water to keep them from perishing. But their supplications were in vain; he most obstinately refused, and thus did they perish. The cry of the children for bread was, as I am informed, so great that it would be impossible for man to describe it.

The foregoing are the principal causes of complaint, and indeed they appear very serious ones to me. However, I having heard those complaints, and understanding that the captain's intention was to take the ship to New York, ... I determined to push on for New York, and there inform the German Society of his conduct. I did so, and on Sunday I found the President of the society. To him I communicated the whole of this disagreeable affair. His feelings can be more easily conceived than described. He, however, gave directions to have the officers of the society summoned to meet the next day, which was done, ...

A GERMAN IN MISSOURI-1820's

The self-sufficiency of the farm unit was one of the attributes of frontier society which impressed Gottfried Duden, an educated German who spent four years (1824-1827) in the new state of Missouri. His account of his residence there was so approving as to attract thousands of his countrymen to settle in Missouri and neighboring Illinois.

(Source: Gottfried Duden, Bericht über eine Reise nach den westlichen Staaten Nordamerika's und einen mehrjahrigen Aufenthalt am Missouri (in den Jahren 1824, 25, 26, und 27), in Bezug auf Auswanderung und Vebervölkerung, St. Gallen, 1832.)

As soon as the emigrating family has reached the site of the new home [in the West] , a halt is made and a fence is built where the buildings are to stand . . . . The choice of a place for the house is determined especially by the neighborhood of a good spring or a brook. Over the spring a small building is at once erected partly to protect it from impurities and partly to preserve the milk, butter, and meat in a cool place.

The next labor is now the building of a dwelling-house. . . . The trunks of the trees are felled in the vicinity and dragged thither by horses or oxen. The house is erected with the help of the neighbors if there are not hands enough in the family. But not more than four or five persons are needed for the erection of a dwelling of this sort. . . .

When the building is completed, and this requires scarcely more than two or three weeks, the family already feels at home; and the next thing on the schedule is to prepare the arable land for agriculture. Usually a man begins by fencing the chosen tract of land in order to use it first as a closed pasture for horses and oxen which one wishes to keep for use nearby.

Nothing can be more erroneous than the European conception of the hardships of converting the forest land into arable land . . . . In criticism of all the descriptions that have been written I merely mention that here, where day labor is paid at the rate of 62 1/2 cents, the whole work on a single field (160 square perches) does not come to more than the small sum of $6, or 15 Dutch gulden . . . . The uprooting of the trees is not to be thought of. Such an undertaking would be laughed at here. Only shrubs and bushes are cleared away by the roots . . . .

Large trees are never cut down. Only trees of one foot or less in diameter are felled, and they are cut so low that the stumps do not disturb the ploughshares. All large trees are merely killed, that is, girdled, cut around into the wood. As a result of the girdling most of them die in about fourteen days so that they draw nothing more from the soil and also no longer shade it. . . .

The cold weather very seldom interrupts the outdoor work for more than two consecutive days. Even in January the weather is not always unfavorable for cutting out the underbrush. The winter cannot be very severe in a place where horses, cows, pigs, not to mention the youngest calves, winter without stables . . . .

As long as the settler does not have sufficient meat from the domestic animals, the hunting grounds keep him in provisions. Flesh of the domestic animals is, to be sure not dear here; a pound of ox flesh costs only 1 1/2 cents and port, 2 cents (3 kreutzer). But there are so many deer, stag, turkeys, hens, pigeons, pheasants, snipes, and other game that a good hunter without much exertion provides for the needs of a large family. Throughout the whole United States, hunting and fishing are entirely free and in the unenclosed spaces anyone can hunt when and how he pleases, small as well as large game, with dogs, nets, slings, and rifles.

There are two varieties of deer here in Missouri, and they are for the most part very fat. The meat is savory, but the hunter seldom takes the whole animal with him. He is satisfied with the hind quarters and the skin, and hangs the rest of the animal on a tree, so that some one else can take home a roast if he wishes. Wild turkeys are found in droves of twenty to fifty. They are especially fat toward Christmas. I have my neighbor deliver some to me every week, especially for soups, for I am not a good hunter. These turkeys must weigh at least 15 pounds or the hunter would not even take them home with him. I pay 12 1/2 cents a piece for them. The bison is no longer to be seen. He has moved farther to the west and north. Bears are still seen occasionally and I hear wolves howling almost every evening. Yet the sheep wander about here without a shepherd, and the farmer suffers as little from wild animals as from robbers and thieves. However, there are complaints that toward the end of April and the middle of May the young pigs are endangered by the she wolves who are rearing their young . . . .

If the planter has two slaves, he can confine himself entirely to duties of inspection without laying his own hand to anything; and the housewife will have just as little to complain of in the work of the household. There is a superfluity of food at hand. Beer also can be easily brewed since hops enough are found in the woods. The apple and peach orchards, which no estate is without, give cider and brandy. Although a very good brandy is also made from corn, yet the brandy from apples and peaches is preferred. I have bought old corn brandy at 30 cents a gallon which came up to the best French brandy. Meanwhile even without slaves the farmer lives in a situation which is infinitely superior to that of a German farmer of the same property. The soil is so productive that the corn crop demands nothing but a mere breaking of the soil, a single ploughing . . . .

Preparation for the next sowing requires the removal of the cornstalks of the previous harvest. These are either cut down, mostly by children, or broken down, then piled together with a harrow and burned. The man who has no harrow makes use very simply of a bunch of branches drawn by one of the horses.

For the sowing of the wheat, rye, and oats less work is likewise required than in Europe. These crops to be sure suffer much from weeds. But an ample supply of land, which does not need to be so carefully used, makes up for this, and European methods of care would here be wasteful of human strength. . . .

A RAPPIST SETTLEMENT-1825

In 1805, Johann Georg Rapp established a religious communitarian settlement in western Pennsylvania. In 1825, Bernhard Karl, Duke of Saxe-Weimar-Eisenach, while traveling through the United States visited this Rappist community, and recorded his observations of the German settlers he saw there. (Source: Bernhard Karl, Reise durch Nord-Amerika in den Jahren 1825 und 1826, Mannheim, Germany, 1827.)

. . . . We visited a Rappist settlement near Pittsburgh. Rapp's principles rest upon community of goods and the cooperation of all members for the common good to insure the welfare of each individual. But Mr. Rapp holds his band together not only by this hope, but also by bonds of religion. It is wonderful that such a simple man should manage to keep together a community of seven-hundred people and influence them to the point that they consider him a prophet. It was, for instance, as a result of his opinion that celibacy was imposed. They found that the community was growing too numerous and agreed to live with their wives in a sisterly relationship. Any more intimate association is forbidden, as is marriage. There were nevertheless a few earlier marriages, and each year a few children are born for whom there is a school and a teacher. All the members feel the greatest respect for Rapp, call him Father, and treat him as one.

They have found that agriculture and cattle raising were not productive enough and have joined to those pursuits a number of industrial enterprises, a cotton and wool factory, a brewery, a distillery, and a grist mill. At a good German lunch we drank a very respectable wine they had made in their old settlement in Ohio.

After our meal we walked about the place, which is laid out in a very orderly fashion. The streets are wide and joined at right angles. It was just two years ago that they began to clear the forest where the settlement now stands; as reminders, the stumps still jut out into the streets. Yet it is astounding how much united and directed human power can accomplish in so short a time.

Some families still live in log houses; but many streets are already occupied with frame houses well set apart from each other, so that each has space for a garden. Only the four-story textile factory, Mr. Rapp's still unfinished home, and a warehouse in process of construction, are made of brick. The log houses are raised in back of the space that will ultimately be taken by the new dwellings. They will in time, then, be able to build new brick structures without disturbing the families that occupy the old ones.

Mr. Rapp's residence seems to testify against that equality of which he preaches, but this seems to arouse no jealousy or hostility. It consists of a two-story main building with two lower wings, and is hung with wallpaper from Philadelphia. Behind the house is a piazza and a balcony which opens out on a garden of several acres, planted with flowers, vegetables, and vines. In the middle is a round basin with a fine fountain. Mr. Rapp wishes to build a little temple there in which to place a statue of Harmony. The statue is already finished, made by a sculptor in Philadelphia out of wood, like the figurehead of a ship.

All the machines in the factory are run by a steam engine of 75 horsepower, made in Pittsburgh; this engine pumps its own water out of a 50 foot well. The factory makes wool and cotton cloth. The community has its own sheep, including some Merinos and some Saxony; but it also buys wool in the neighborhood from farmers who now begin to concern themselves with sheep-raising. After the wool is washed it is picked by the oldest women in the community, who work on the fourth floor, and then it is sent down to the lower floors through a kind of funnel. The wool is sorted into four groups according to quality, and dyed in their own dye-house near the factory. It is then brought back to the factory where it is combed and spun thinner and thinner into fine threads on machines like the Jenny. Once spun, it is woven and then fulled on a machine operated by steam.

In the winter, heat is supplied through pipes that lead off the steam engine and extend to every story of the building. All the workers, and especially the women, had very healthy complexions, and the sincere friendship with which they greeted Rapp moved me deeply. I was also pleased to find vases of fresh flowers near all the machines, and everywhere was a praiseworthy cleanliness.

After visiting this interesting factory we went for tea to Mr. Rapp's temporary dwelling, a good frame house. Here I met his daughter, a pale spinster, and a blooming granddaughter, Gertraud, child of an only son whose death made a deep impression on the old man. The table was set with fine silver, and Rapp seemed pleased to be able to show me the degree of his prosperity. He started out, as he himself told me, with very slight means; in the beginning he had to struggle with the bitterest want and not seldom had to seek bread for his community. . . .

The next morning we continued our tour of the settlement. We inspected the distillery which turns out fine whiskey well esteemed in the neighborhood, although there was no need for it in the community itself for the members had convenanted with each other to make no use of spirituous liquors. . . .

On every floor of the mill and of the other factory buildings are great iron tanks filled with water so that there will always be at hand the means of extinquishing fires. The community also has its own fire engine and a company to man it.

The articles for the use of the members are kept separately. There is no private property and everything belongs to the community, which must provide the individuals with all the things they need. The cloth for clothing is of the best quality, as are the provisions. Flour, salt, fish, and other goods that keep for a long time are distributed to the families monthly; fresh meat and other articles that spoil easily are distributed, according to the size of the family, more frequently. Since every house has a garden, each family may raise its own vegetables and fowl, and each bakes its own bread. For articles which are not made in the community itself, there is a store from which members may draw on an order by the directors, and in which outsiders from the neighborhood may buy. . . .

THE GREAT ENGINEER-1831

Johann August Roebling, an engineer from Berlin, came to the United States in 1831. He became one of the greatest bridge builders in American history. This selection is an extract from his Diary describing his journey to America, and his first impressions of his newly adopted country.
(Source: Johann August Roebling, Diary of My Journey (Trenton, New Jersey, 1931.)

Today we journeyed from Muehlhausen, took leave of our friends, relatives and acquaintances, and said farewell to our native plain, in the hope of establishing a new home, a new Fatherland which will treat us indeed as a father, in the western continent, beyond the Atlantic Ocean . . . We are not going with exaggerated views or extravagant hopes. To what extent America corresponds with our moderate expectations and affords us what we seek, the future must teach . . . .

The impression, which the populace has made on me, has turned out more favourably than I had expected . . . . The outward demeanor of the people or of the townsfolk, and their public conduct is more modest here and at the same time more free and unconstrained than I have noticed in any important city in Germany . . . . Nowhere does one see a person in rags; all, even the common workmen go very cleanly and neatly dressed . . .

We have altered our previous opinion regarding the Southern States. In consequence of this we have made our decision to settle in a free State. Here one is universally prejudiced against the slaveholding States and that with right.

The Northern states criticize the Southern ones very much, and it is neigher lying nor dissembling, and in this all reasonable Americans agree, to say that slavery is the greatest cancerous affliction from which the United States are suffering. Slavery contrasts too greatly with the rest of their political and civic institutions. The republic is branded by it and the entire folk with its idealistic and altogether purely reasonable Constitution, stands branded by it before the eyes of the civilized world. Grounds enough for us not to go into any slave-holding State, even if Nature had created a Paradise there!

Let one inquire about the gigantic construction of the New York Canal, the Ohio Canal, the multitude of smaller canals, roads and railways, and the German wonders how all this could have been accomplished without first having had an army of governmental counsellors, ministers and other functionaries deliberate about it for ten years, make numerous expensive journeys by post, and write so many reports about it that for the amount expended for all this, reckoning compound interest for ten years, the work could have been completed . . . .

A SHOPKEEPER IN CINCINNATI-1835

Gustavus Wulfing had been an inkeeper in Germany. He came to the United States in 1835, tried farming in the Ohio Valley, and then opened a small jewelry shop in the highly German city of Cincinnati. This selection is an excerpt of his description of his life in the Queen City of the West.

(Source: J. M. Wulfing, ed., Gustavus Wulfing: Letters, Fulton, Ohio, 1941.)

I soon realized that farming was not the right thing for us. I did not get a chance to learn the language and customs; I had to work and sweat all day . . . to raise enough for our needs. We decided to return to Cincinnati, and I started a small jewelry business by myself. With the aid of our Lord I hope to earn enough to make a living for us and to be able to put a few dollars aside. I intend to import jewelry from Germany and am convinced that I can make money. Christiane is happy that we gave up the much-praised country life. She was always by herself. Here she can visit the Backhaus family . . . with whom we are well acquainted. We were fortunate to find a nice and comfortable home, and I have learned English so well that I am able to transact business . . . .

We have three German churches here---a Catholic, an Evangelical, and a Lutheran, and each church has a school of its own. We joined the Lutheran church, as we liked the pastor best. The Evangelical minister operates a flour mill, and also a blacksmith shop . . . . All churches--- German or English---are heated. Our pastor gets a salary of about six hundred dollars per year, and three hundred dollars will cover his living expenses if managed wisely. There are several printing establishments and two Germna-language newspapers; also two companies of German militiamen to protect the city in cas of need . . . .

We live about the same way as in Germany. In the morning we have coffee, wheat bread, and butter; at noon a piece of meat, which is better and cheaper than in Germany, with potatoes and cabbage---on Sundays soup, and in the evening coffee or tea. Christiane takes care of the household and of the children, who often play . . . "grandmother and aunt"---and I attend to my business. In the evening, when the children are in bed, I read to Christy from the Bible, or Hasenkamp's Letters, or something else. Sunday mornings Christy and I alternate in going to church. There is no church in the afternoon, and we spend our time visiting the Backhaus or the Pauck family, or they call on us, and we serve coffee, bread, and butter.

When the weather is bad we stay at home and pass the time by talking about our beloved ones who stayed in Germany, about this country, or our dangerous and troublesome trip, or our experiences on the farm, etc; and our conversation will always wind up with: "Our Lord guided us well, He protected and shielded us from danger and injury, and He showed us immeasurable kindness which far exceeded our comprehension." The many fine German books which we brought with us give us much pleasure, and we realize now what a great treasure they represent . . .

Generally speaking, a merchant must have capital to be successful in Germany. In this country the lack of money can be overcome by a spirit of enterprise and by diligence; and respectable conduct is frequently all that is needed to get credit. Fritz, as well as I, could buy a stock worth a thousand dollars on credit terms. I do not like to make use of this, as I prefer to do business in a small way; I pay cash for all purchases and this will give me a good credit-rating. German penny-pinchers are not known; Americans do not worry much about the future. If a fellow has only one dollar left, he does not mind spending it, as most people feel that tomorrow will take care of itself; they can work a day and this will give them money to cover their needs.

To do business is not very difficult when you know the American ways. I earned six dollars yesterday. A few days ago I happened to be in a coffee house and heard that the owner wanted to buy goods for which he was willing to pay twelve dollars. I knew where to get these for seven dollars on the same street. I bought the goods for him, took a roundabout way, delivered the same and made five dollars profit in about fifteen minutes. Of course this does not happen every day, but there are similar chances every hour of the day; more than once I could not find time to eat lunch . . . .

I am pleased that Julius wants to come to America. I assure you that it is my honest opinion that he will do better in this country than he would in Germany, even if someone should give him a thousand Taler on the condition that he stay. If he becomes a teacher he would be lucky to earn after many years as much as three hundred Taler per annum, and if he were fortunate enough to earn more, the entire country would talk about such unheard of luck; if he is not inclined to become a teacher, even a still higher salary would not make him happy.

If he wishes to become a merchant, he would have to go into a hardware store, or some other store, and he would have to pass through an apprenticeship of four to six years, and then serve as a soldier; or, if he is not subject to army service, he would be a humble traveling salesman or an office attendant until he succeeds enough, by exercising the greatest thrift, to start a small store, etc. He would not be able to help his brother, no matter how hard he tried; and Friedrich would have to go through the same struggle to be able to earn a living. If the two boys wish, or are compelled, to stay in Germany, I would advise them to learn a good old-fashioned trade, simply because I know from my own experience what opportunities a merchant without capital has in Germany. Think this over most carefully and tell it to all concerned.

If Julius comes to America this summer, I shall give him room and board besides fifty dollars or more the first year, and we shall treat him as our own child. As soon as I get his answer and the consent of his guardian, I shall send $100.00 and letters of recommendation, and I shall give him complete instructions about the best way to make the trip. If he makes up his mind to come, he should make every effort to learn English. By the time Friedrich is confirmed, Julius will have saved enough to loan him $100.00, so that he can come to this country too, and in this way he would be a great help to his younger brother . . . .

GERMAN PAUPERS-1836

As immigration to the United States from the German states increased, the United States government became alarmed at the growing numbers of German paupers arriving at American ports. However, letters from American consuls in Germany reported that there was no conscious effort on the part of the German governments to send their poor to the New World.
(Source: "Report from the Secretary of the Treasury, Relative to the Deportation of Paupers from Great Britain, etc., in Obedience to the Resolution of the Senate of the 4th of July, 1836," U. S. 24th Congress, 2nd Session, Senate Document, No. 5.)

From the United States Consulate at Bremen (letter of September 5, 1836):

. . . . . I am sorry that the information desired is not to be procured from authentic sources; for, properly speaking, it cannot be said that paupers are deported from Germany, though it may sometimes (but very rarely) be the case that families, almoners, and civil authorities, in order to get rid of a burdensome fellow or troublesome subject, pay what is necessary for such a person to cross the Atlantic. But, among the German emigrants, a great number of which annually embark at this port, and who nearly all go the the United States, there are many persons and families, who, when they have paid for the passage, have little or no money left, and probably many of them, on arriving in the United States, are quite destitute of all. The different Governments of Germany are, in general, not much pleased with the spirit of emigration since several years predominant in Germany, and, as is said, try by all means to keep their subjects at home. The emigrants very often loudly and bitterly complain that the said Governments, before they give to people the permission to depart, put as many obstacles as possible in the way of persons who intend to emigrate. Such emigrants, as I hear, must usually prove to their Governments that they have money enough to pay for their travelling expenses and for their passage, the said Governments being afraid that the emigrants may, by travelling uselessly, spend their little fortune, and then return and come on the charge of the community; and the emigrants are therefore obliged to renounce and give up all their rights as natives of the country. After the emigrants have got the permission to emigrate, and set out, then their former Governments do not further care for them . . . . .

From the United States Consulate at Hesse Cassel (letter of September 8, 1836):

. . . . As far as I have been able to ascertain, none of the German Governments have caused, or even indirectly sanctioned, any deportation of their paupers; on the contrary, their laws and finances forbid such operation.

The only forced deportation which has come to my knowledge, is from the free Hanseatic town of Hamburg, the Government of which deports, from time to time, those criminals which have been either condemned for life or a long period; they give them the choice either to endure their time or to emigrate; in which case the Government pays their passage. A number of them have been sent to New York, and this year to Brazil.

The great number of German paupers in the United States arises from the low rate of passage-money which of late had existed. Steerage passengers were taken last spring from Bremen, and found with good provisions, at $16 each grown person. This price the Bremen shipowners could only afford by carrying always a large number, to obtain which they had their agents all over in the interior of Germany, and induced the lower class, which live in a very impoverished state, to emigrate, by making them believe that labor was so much demanded in the United States that any able-bodied man could earn, as soon as landed, $2 a day. Young and old, healthy and sickly, thought now of nothing but to emigrate; every sacrifice was made, even their clothes were sold, and if this did not suffice, the balance begged; and all those who could scrape together enough to pay their passage went to the United States, where the majority landed penniless, and a great number of them, consisting of old people, women, and children, unable to work, as the German Government does not allow their young men to emigrate . . . .

GERMANS GO WEST--1836

No improvement in transportation had a greater impact than the Erie Canal. Among other things, it facilitated immigrant movement westward to the northern portions of the Old Northwest. A newly arrived German immigrant, Jacob Schramm, who made the journey in 1836, recorded his experiences in letters to his family. (Source: Emma S. Vonnegut, ed., "The Schramm Letters: Written by Jacob Schramm and Members of His Family from Indiana to Germany in the year 1836," Indiana Historical Society Publications, XII, #4, Indianapolis, 1935.)

We arranged for the trip to Buffalo in a canalboat: sleeping quarters, and meals with the captain, 8 dollars each. This is a distance of 360 English miles, or 72 German ones, and the trip lasted 7 days. The boats are suitably fitted up. There are three cabins: a small one where the women passengers sleep; a second, with benches, which at night are put together and made into beds for the men; and a third where meals are served. Next to the dining room is the kitchen, where the sailors and the cook have their quarters. In the middle is the large space for goods. The boats are not very large, about 50 feet long and 10 wide, with the lower deck just high enough so a man can stand upright; nevertheless everything is surprisingly well managed. People of this region, therefore, make constant use of these boats, and it never occurs to anyone to go by foot, to ride, or travel by carriage. If one wants to live cheaply he can, if he takes care of his own provisions. In that case a person pays just half for the trip, and is allowed 50 lbs. free. When we went aboard this canalboat at Albany it was already nightfall; still, goods and people were being taken on and continued to be until 11 o'clock. Everything was weighed. The passengers who boarded themselves went into the back room, but those who ate with us at the captain's table, into the cabin itself. . . .

That night the boat lay at Albany, and in the morning it was taken into the lock and weighed; then the canal toll was paid. How high the amount was, I could not discover, with my lack of English, but the toll must stand at such a figure in relation to the freight rates as to allow profit to the boat owners, the shippers, and the state of New York, which built the canal, for there is a tremendous, continuous line of boats coming and going; indeed, as I learned later in German, the canal is long since paid for, and now has a big balance.

The weighing of the boat was done in this fashion. The boat is taken into a lock, which has the same water level as the canal and is an extension of it. When the boat is at the right spot, the entrance to the lock from the canal is closed by a gate that reaches the bottom, and fits so tight that no water can come through. The lock is then opened on the other side so that the water runs out. When it is out, the boat rests on a scaffold connected with big scales above, and in 5 minutes the weighing is finished. Thereupon the lock is again opened so that the water can rush back. In a few minutes it is back as it was before, and the boat returns to the canal.

The boat is drawn by horses, usually in relays of two, and day and night they keep up a sharp pace. The canal is only 4 or 5 feet deep, and of course the boats are built in accordance. For the most part they are the property of companies in New York or Albany, or other cities along the way, and have connections at all the landings. There are companies that have 300 such boats, which continually take goods and people to the western states, and bring produce to the eastern states. This output from the interior consists chiefly of cornmeal, barley, tobacco, and hides. There are also people who use the canals independently, but they cannot take passengers, because they have to have their own horses with them all the way. When one pair is tired, they are brought aboard and fed while the other team is hitched to the boat, and so they alternate. Every boat has to have a man to drive the horses. The companies that have so many boats have farms at different stations, where they keep a large number of horses, and where the horses are changed and fresh drivers provided. There are also many mail packets, likewise company owned, which expedite light packages, letters and passengers. They are narrower and longer than freight boats, and constructed less for heavy loads than for speed. A trip can be made very quickly on one of these, for the horses keep at a trot as they do with a German express, but they are more expensive.

The first day we traveled through beautiful, settled country, with the Mohawk River, which by means of locks supplies the water for the middle section of the canal, on the right. It is a good-sized stream, but hasn't enough water for steamships. Beyond are heavily wooded mountains, and the whole view is splendid. Along the canal is a chain of inns and stores where a person can get in one place what, in Germany, he would have to look for in many shops and workshops.

The first day we passed many locks, and that delayed the trip. The canal is for the most part laid out where the country is flattest, but as all the hills cannot be avoided, locks have to be built, which must cost frightful sums. There are perhaps 200 between Albany and Buffalo. At the entrance into one of these locks, built from quarried stone, there is a pair of gates, which is closed when the boat is once inside. The upper section of the canal, perhaps 10 or 15 feet higher, is held by another gate, which is closed while one is going through the lower gate, and then opened as soon as the lower one is closed. As the water comes rushing through the gate of the lock, the water and the boat at the closed door are lifted, rising to the height of the upper level. This process is repeated till one is up the hill. Sometimes the rise is small, and only 1 or 2 such locks are needed but sometimes it is greater, and 4, 6, 8, 10, or even 12 locks follow one after the other. The boat that wants to descend must wait meanwhile until the lock gate of the lower level is opened . . . . .

So the journey proceeded as far as Buffalo, which we reached Sunday morning at three o'clock.

A NOVELIST LOOKS AT GERMAN EMIGRANTS-1837

Herman Melville, the great novelist, spent a few weeks in Liverpool in 1837, where he saw German emigrants embarking for America. He was so stirred by the scene, that, when he wrote his semi-autobiographical novel Redburn, he described the scene in moving prose that seemed to capture the meaning of America for these Germans as well as for humanity.
(Source: Herman Melville, Redburn, New York, 1849.)

. . . . There was hardly anything I witnessed in the docks that interested me more than the German immigrants who come on board the large New York ships several days before their sailing, to make everything comfortable ere starting. Old men, tottering with age, and little infants in arms; laughing girls in bright-buttoned bodices, and astute, middle-aged men with pictured pipes in their mouths, would be seen mingling together in crowds of five, six and seven or eight hundred in one ship.

Every evening these countrymen of Luther and Melancthon gathered on the forecastle to sing and pray. And it was exalting to listen to their fine ringing anthems, reverberating among the crowded shipping, and rebounding from the lofty walls of the docks. Shut your eyes, and you would think you were in a cathedral.

There is something in the contemplation of the mode in which America has been settled, that, in a noble breast, should forever extinguish the prejudices of national dislikes . . . .

Emigration from Germany included not only fugitives from famine, but also farmers and artisans with enough funds to start life in in the United States, and a few political refugees. A writer in a British periodical described the early stages of that movement. (Source: Chamber's Edinburgh Journal, V, June 13, 1846.)

Germany is the only other country, besides Great Britain, from which emigration takes place on a great scale, and is likely to lead to important results. Since the year 1840, she has sent out annually 60,000 settlers, about our own average. In the present year [1846] , the number is stated in the English papers at 80,000. It is very probable that this number will continue for the future, and even increase, as the predisposing causes are not occasional, but permanent, in the subsisting state of the country. The reasons which are all-powerful there, are not the same as actuate us. The results, too are very different . . . .

The chief emigration to America at present is from the Upper and Middle Rhine, the Grand Duchy of Baden, Wurtemberg, the two Hesses, and Bavaria. In Bavaria especially, whole village communities sell their property for whatever they can get, and set out, with their clergyman at their head. "It is a lamentable sight," says a French writer, "when you are travelling in the spring or autumn on the Strasburg road, to see the long files of carts that meet you every mile, carrying the whole property of the poor wretches, who are about to cross the Atlantic on the faith of a lying prospectus. There they go slowly along; their miserable tumbrils ---drawn by such starved, drooping beasts, that your only wonder is, how they can possibly hope to reach Havre alive---piled with the scanty boxes containing their few effects, and on the top of all, the women and children, the sick and bedridden, and all who are too exhausted with the journey to walk.

One might take it for a convoy of wounded, the relics of a battlefield, but for the rows of little white heads peeping from beneath the ragged hood." These are the emigrants from Bavaria and the Upper Rhine, who have no seaport nearer than Havre. Those from the north of Germany, who are comparatively few in number, sail mostly from Bremen. The number of these likewise is increasing. From 1832 to 1835 inclusive, 9,000 embarked every year from Bremen; from 1839 to 1842, the average number was 13,000; which increased to 19,000 in the year 1844.

Society in Germany is so much more rudimentary than in England, that it is remarkable to see this same tendency exhibiting itself in the two nations. In Germany population is comparatively sparse, in Great Britain it is dense; in the one there is great wealth and profound poverty, in the other the extremes of property rarely exist; the one has a large and dominant town population, the other has fewer towns in proportion than any country in Europe; the one teems with political activity, in the other political activity is not, or at least has not yet taken to itself a practical presence and a name.

The dread of destitution is a motive to emigrate in Germany, as in England; but not a principal motive. This is clear from the fact that the emigration does not take place in those districts where there is most want, but exists equally where population is dense, and where it is thinly distributed. In Westphalia, for instance, a great number of small proprietors have lately sold their lands, and sailed for America--each of whom, it is reckoned, has taken with him at least thirty pounds' worth of goods and money. The Bavarians emigrate alike from the Rhine country, where population is thickly clustered together, and from the upland districts, where there are not eighty inhabitants to the square mile.

The one great cause of this almost national movement is the desire for absolute political and religious freedom; the absence of all restrictions upon the development of society; and the publication of opinions which cannot be realized at home. The great agitation in society, caused first by the French domination, and then by the convulsive rise against it, has never passed away. In that gigantic struggle, when everything rested on the popular soul, the bonds of privilege and class were tacitly abandoned, and could never thenceforth be reunited as before. The promises of having constitutional governments, at that time made by the sovereigns to their subjects, have been but partially fulfilled. There is nothing that can be called oppression on the part of the government; . . . but there are many restrictions, and the young, the restless, and the imaginative thirst for their ideal freedom, and many of them seek for the realization of Utopia in America.

Complete religious equality is a still more powerful want in a country where Catholics and Protestants are so nearly balanced, and where the state of parties is such, that the minority in faith, though nominally equal in law, must always live under the cold shade of an alien creed. This of itself has urged many across the Atlantic . . . .

Another motive has been the great success of some of the earlier settlers. The Moravians and Shakers, who have emigrated from Germany, have worked wonders in some parts. In 1815, the Separatists, another religious body, sometimes called Rappists, from their head, M. Rapp, sailed from Wurtemberg with a capital only of £1,200, and formed a settlement on the Ohio. At the present time, the real property in land belonging to the society is reckoned at £ 340,000, exclusive of personal property, and a large sum of money in the funds. The success of the colony of Zoar has been equally striking. It was founded twenty years ago by a few families with a scanty capital, and now possesses 40,000 acres of land, a disposable capital of £ 100,000 and an immense quantity of machinery and stock, foundries, tan-pits, and mills in abundance. This extraordinary affluence is because these two colonies were founded on the principle of a community of property, and have been throughout under a strict religious government. But the present emigrants forget this; and looking only at the prosperity achieved, they think that as the Moravians and Rappists have succeeded, they must succeed to the same extent, without either the same capital or self-denial.

EMIGRATION OF GERMAN PAUPERS-1847

German paupers continued to come to America even after the Federal government made some attempts to stop their inflow. New York City was especially inundated with these peoples. This selection is an extract from a report sent to Congress by the New York City government relative to the problem.
(Source: "Memorial to Congress from the corporation of the city of New York Relative to the Exportation from Abroad of Paupers and Criminals," U. S. 29th Congress, 2nd Session, House Document No. 54, January 25, 1847.)

. . . . Your memorialists further represent, that large numbers of paupers are sent every year to this country from the poor-houses of Europe, and for the sole reason that it is much cheaper to pay their passage to this country than to support them at home. Those sent are the diseased infirm, and helpless portion of the community, who, when they arrive, can be of no benefit to our country, and remain inmates of our alms-house. Within the last year, two vessels---the ships "Sardinia" and "Atlas," from Liverpool---arrived in this port, one with 294, and the other with 314, steerage passengers, all of whom were paupers, sent by the parish of Grosszimmern, in Hesse Darmstadt, to which they belonged, and the expenses of which were paid by said parish.

Your memorialists cannot consider the paupers sent here from the poorhouses of Europe as emigrants, or worthy of that name, and would suggest that a representation of the facts be made through our ministers and consuls to the foreign governments from which paupers are sent; and your memorialists call the special attention of Congress to the copies of letters from the parishes of Hall and Grosszimmern, hereto annexed . . . . .

The Overseers of the Hospital and the Poor at Hall to the Local Authorities of Grosszimmern, in Darmstadt [May 5] : . . . . .
"We learn that a considerable number of emigrants will, within a few weeks, proceed from the neighboring parish of Grosszimmern, on their voyage to America. It is an emigration of the poorer class, who are without the means of gaining a livelihood, as already has been partially done in Ireland at the public expense. In this case, the parish of Grosszimmern defrays the charges, and besides providing for these rather numerous paupers on their passage across the ocean, places at their disposition the means of supplying the wants of the moment, on their arrival at the North American coast.

"In the parish here, is also unfortunately a number of paupers, by no means inconsiderable, of both the male and female sex; and we are not disinclined to adopt similar means to those which you found suited to your design; for which reason, information is respectfully requested on the following points: First, how the thing was managed; second, with whom the bargain for transportation was made; third, how many persons were

sent off; fourth, how much was paid and, fifth, how much was appropri-
ated for their first wants on the other side of the sea. Persuaded of
your friendly disposition, the undersigned believe they have made no
vain request; and offering to reciprocate the service, look respectfully
for the desired communication."

The answer of the burgomaster of Grosszimmern followed on the
first of September, 1846, and reads thus:

"The Board of Overseers of the Hospital and the Poor will not mis-
construe the circumstance that their esteemed letter of the eleventh of
last month did not receive an earlier reply. Now, however, that the many
labors which became necessary on account of the emigrants in question
are in some degree lightened, I hasten to impart the following explanations
concerning the questions put to me. To the first question: This parish,
which numbers four thousand inhabitants, comprehends so many who have
not the least property, that it was no longer possible for them to support
themselves and their families.

"In consequence of letters received last year from emigrants from
this place, in which it was said that in North America, on account of the
cheapness of the means of subsistence, laborers, and especially such as
were able to assist in field labors, made good earnings, the wish arose in
many of our inhabitants of the poorer class to be aided in reaching North
America by the funds of the parish. The local authorities availed themselves of this opportunity, and issued a public invitation to all such poor
persons as of their own free motion desired to emigrate to America, to apply to the burgomaster. Hereupon a list was made out, arranged under
the following titles, to wit: 1st, number of the emigrant; 2d, his name;
3d, statement of the members of his family and parents; 4th, amount of
his property; 5th, his wants, both for the expenses of the journey and clothing; 6th, remarks.

"To question second: For the passage, a bargain was made with Mr.
Gansenberg, at Darmstadt, and Mr. Grulen, Gernsheim, by whom it was
executed to our full satisfaction.

"To question third: There were 674 persons sent off at the expense of
the parish, besides more than a hundred who emigrated with them at their
own charge.

"To question fourth: For each person over twelve years old, 71
florins were paid for passage and board; but for each person under twelve,
56 florins from Gernsheim to New York, including the capitation and poor
tax there to be paid, which amounts to about two florins and 24 kreutzers.

"To the fifth question: Each family that was large received a bill of
exchange of from 15 to 25 florins, drawn upon the house of Speyer, in
New York. This was handed to the emigrants in London by one of the
local authorities who accompanied them thither.

"The parish had to take up a sum amounting nearly to 50,000 florins,
for which, it is true, that the titles of the emigrants to the undivided lands
of the parishes were made over. It may be asked whether the parish has
lost or gained. Aside from the considerable sum of ready money which
in this manner is withdrawn from us, the parish has at all events gained . . .

One of the largest and most influential of all the various immigrant organizations was the German Society of New York. This selection describes some of their activities and complaints. (Source: "Memorial of the Officers of the German Society of the City of New York to the New York State Legislature, Demanding a Share of the Head Tax Receipts," New York Assembly Document, No. 165, 1848.)

The memorial of the undersigned officers of the German Society of the city of New York respectfully showeth:

That the immigration from Germany at this port during the last year, was greater than that from any other country, while the expenditures arising therefrom, which had to be borne by the Commissioners of Emigration, were trifling in comparison with the great burden thrown upon said Commissioners by the immigration from other countries.

According to the report of said Commissioners, submitted to the Honorable the Legislature of the State of New York, there arrived at this port from the 5th of May to the 31st of December, 1847, 129,069 immigrant passengers, of whom 53,180 were natives of Germany, 52,946 were natives of Germany, 52,946 were natives of Ireland and 22,943 were natives of other countries.

The number of those who became chargeable to the Commissioners was 10,422 and the amount expended for their support was, from the commutation fund, $65,317.44; from the hospital fund, $82,829.87; in all, $148,147.31. Which sum, divided by the above number of those for whose sake it was expended, say 10,422, shows the average cost of each to have been $14.21 1/2.

The report of the Commissioners does not state distinctly how many of said 10,422 persons whom they had to support were Germans, inasmuch as it includes 3,416 persons admitted into the marine hospital from ship board, without mentioning places of nativity; but your memorialists believe the Germans among said 3,416 persons were proportionately not more numerous than among those sent to the hospital from the city. The number thus sent was 2,802, of whom 196 were Germans; hence, of the 3,416 admitted from ship board, 238 were Germans. Adding these 238 to the number enumerated as natives of Germany, in Table B, appended to the Report of the Commissioners of Emigration, it appears that the total number of Germans, who became chargeable to the Commissioners, out of an immigration of 53,180, was 872.

Your memorialists feel confident that this estimate is quite large enough and that they may safely refer to the Commissioners of Emigration themselves for the correctness of this view. In fact the latter will readily admit that the patients sent to the marine hospital from ship board were almost exclusively natives of Ireland, and assuming 238 to have been Germans, is a larger number than should fairly be allowed. But your memorialists desire to be on the safe side, and prefer, if err they must to do so to their own disadvantage.

Your Honorable Body is aware that the tax collected from emigrant passengers is one dollar from each, commutation money, and fifty cents from each, hospital money. Hence the money collected from 53,180 Germans, at $1.50 each, is $79,770.00. The expenditures for the support of 872 Germans, who became chargeable, at $14,21 1/2 each, is $12,395.48. And thus the surplus of receipts over expenditures of the German immigration at this port, is $67,374.52.

The number of immigrants, other than Germans was 75,889, and the hospital and commutation money collected from them, at $1.50 each, was $113,833.50. Of these 75,889 immigrants, 9,550 became chargeable to the Commissioners, at a cost of $14.21 1/2 each, amounting in the aggregate to $135,753.25, showing an excess of expenditures over receipts of $21,919.75.

Thus then it is shown by the Report of the Commissioners of Emigration that the receipts from immigrant passengers, natives of Germany, overran the expenditure caused by the same, $67,374.52, while on the other hand the receipts from the immigrants from other countries a loss of $21,919.75.

This result is no doubt principally owing to the fact that the immigrants from Germany arrived in better condition than the great mass of those from other countries, but it would be incorrect to take this fact as a full and satisfactory explanation of the remarkable disparity. Your memorialists feel convinced, and beg leave to show, that in a great degree it is brought about by the working of the German Society.

The German immigrant, on his arrival here, if he requires assistance, does not call on the Commissioners of Emigration, but at the place where his native language is spoken, he calls on the German Society; and the German Society does not send him to the office of the Commissioners (except in extraordinary cases) because the Commissioners have made it a rule to grant relief only in their own institutions. But ample proof is daily furnished by the visitors of our Society, that it is next to impossible to induce the German immigrant voluntarily to become an inmate of those institutions; he will rather submit to actual suffering, and thus, ignorance of the language of the country, and the dread of the alms-house, which the German looks upon as a sort of penitentiary, throw the chief burden of the indigent German immigration on the German Society, and the latter, by the force of a portion of the expenses, which, by the act of May 5, 1847, "concerning passengers in vessels coming to the city of New York," are intended to fall on the Commissioners of Emigration. For the truth of this, your memorialists may confidently refer to the Commissioners themselves.

The enormous immigration at this port from Germany, which, during the year of 147, according to the books kept at the office of the German Society, amounted to 70,735 persons, proves a serious burden to the citizens of German origin. It will be readily admitted that among such a mass of people there must be many having neither friends nor relatives among the resident Germans, but requiring medical as well as pecuniary assistance.

As already stated, the suffering and needy will in the first place apply to the German Society, but failing to receive all the aid they require, they will throw themselves, not on the Commissioners of Emigration, but on the sympathy of their countrymen, and these cannot possibly resist the appeal. Hence it is that the indigent and suffering German immigration proves a constant and daily increasing tax upon all the resident Germans, and this explains the circumstance, that out of 10,000 German voters, only about 500 are members of the German Society. It is not an unfriendly feeling towards the society which prevents so many from joining the same, but the consciousness of doing enough without contributing towards its funds. On the other hand, the society feels keenly the absence of that general co-operation which it would enjoy, but for the reasonable objection urged by so many of its well wishers.

There are now 58 persons actively engaged in carrying on the business of the society, viz: 15 members of the executive council, 17 physicians, 24 district visitors and 2 employees in the agency office. The services of all are gratuitous, with the exception of the agent and his clerk, who receive salaries. The total expenditures during the last twelve months was $7,823.10, which sufficed to afford substantial and adequate relief to 3,721 deserving applicants, while the agency procured employment to 4,743 persons. Your memorialists would say that it would be impossible to accomplish a greater amount of good with equally limited means.

There is one channel through which the German Society is constantly endeavoring to extend the sphere of its benevolent action, which your memorialists take leave to notice more particularly. This is an arrangement with the regular German physicians of New York and Brooklyn, now numbering about twenty, by which the latter are represented in the board of officers of the society, and take charge of all the sick German poor, attending them gratuitously, the society paying for medicines, nurses, etc. According to the last annual report of the society, its physicians, during the last twelve months, prescribed medicines in 2,808 cases, and had under treatment, for account of the society, 714 patients. Considering that the inmates of the hospitals under the control of the Commissioners of Emigration cost $14.21 1/2 each, it will not be deemed extravagant on the part of your memorialists to say that the medical department of the German Society has saved the city and the Commissioners of Emigration many thousand dollars.

But the extraordinary exertions made by the society during the last twelve months have exhausted its means and it is now threatened with the prospect of having to suspend its usefulness. Your memorialists, therefore, compelled by the embarrassing condition of the society, and in consideration of its being so efficient an auxilliary to the Commissioners of Emigration, venture to ask your honorable body for aid, and they also venture to hope their prayer will be satisfactorily responded to on the ground that the German immigrant, as shown in the beginning of this "Memorial," has not derived the same amount of benefit from the operation of the act of May 5, 1847, as the emigrant from other countries, having in fact furnished the means by which not his own wants but those of others have been relieved.

It is not the intention of your memorialists, nor the object of their prayer, to relieve the members of the German Society from the claims on them of their poor countrymen; on the contrary, your memorialists wish to keep alive, and if possible, to enlarge the springs of private charity; and the prayer of your memorialists is this:

That an act be passed requiring the Commissioners of Emigration to pay to the treasurer of the German Society for its use, the sum of----- dollars, and further authorizing aid commissioners to pay annually to said treasurer on or before the 1st of March of every year an amount equal to one-half the sum of voluntary contributions, collected during the preceding twelve months from the members of said society, so long as said commissioners can satisfy themselves that the German Society has a fair claim to such support, and provided, also, that such annual payment shall not exceed the sum of $3,000; these payments to be made out of the Commutation Fund.

"KLEINDEUTSCHLAND"-1850'S

The German element was a very conspicuous ingredient of New York City in the 1850's. By the eve of the Civil War, a majority of the city's some 120,000 German-born residents appear to have been concentrated in the section from Houston to Twelfth Street, eastward from the Bowery. This "Deutschländle, or "Little Germany," was described by Karl Theodor Griesinger, a member of the German liberal generation of the forties.
(Source: Karl Theodor Griesinger, Land und Leute in America: Skizzen ausdem amerikanischen Leben, 2 vols. (Stuttgart, 1863.)

The traveller who passes up Broadway, through Chatham Street, into the Bowery, up Houston Street, and thence right to First Avenue will find himself in a section which has very little in common with the other parts of New York. The arrangement of the streets and the monotony of the brownstone dwellings are similar, but the height and detail of the houses, the inhabitants, and their language and customs differ greatly from those of the rest of New York. This is "Kleindeutschland," or "Deutschlandle," as the Germans call this part of the city . . . . .

The first floor of the houses along these avenues serves as a grocery or shoemaker's shop, or even an inn; but the upper floors still house from five to 24 families, in some buildings as many as 48. . . . On each floor of such buildings there are eight apartments, four on the street side and four on the back. Naturally the apartments are very small: a living room with two windows and a bedroom with no windows---that is all. The room with the two windows is 10 feet by 10 feet, and such apartments rent for five to six dollars a month. Apartments in buildings where only ten or twelve families reside rent for eight to nine dollars. These apartments contain a comfortable living room, with three windows, and two bedrooms. According to the standards of the German workingman, one can live like a prince for ten to fourteen dollars a month. Apartments at this price contain two bedrooms, two living rooms, one of which is used for a kitchen, and sufficient room for storing coal and wood.

That's how the Germans live in Kleindeutschland. But they are satisfied-happy, contented, and, most significantly, among their own people . . . Deutschländle certainly deserves its name, because 15,000 German families, comprising seventy to seventy-five thousand people live here. New York has about 120,000 German born inhabitants. Two-thirds of these live in Kleindeutschland. They come from every part of Germany, although those from northern Germany are rarer than those from the southern part, and Hessians people from Baden, Wuertembergers, and Rhenish Bavarians are most numerous.

117

Naturally the Germans were not forced by the authorities, or by law, to settle in this specific area. It just happened. But the location was favorable because of its proximity to the downtown business district where the Germans are employed. Moreover, the Germans like to live together; this permits them to speak their own language and live according to their own customs. The cheapness of the apartments also prompted their concentration. As the first Germans came into Kleindeutschland, the Irish began to move and the Americans followed because they were ashamed to live among immigrants.

Life in Kleindeutschland is almost the same as in the Old Country. Bakers, butchers, druggists-all are Germans. There is not a single business which is not run by Germans. Not only the shoemakers, tailors, barbers, physicians, grocers, and innkeepers are German, but the pastors and priests as well. There is even a German lending library where one can get all kinds of German books. The resident of Kleindeutschland need not even know English in order to make a living, which is a considerable attraction to the immigrant.

The shabby apartments are the only reminder that one is in America. Tailors or shoemakers use their living rooms as workshops, and there is scarcely space to move about. The smell in the house is not too pleasant, either, because the bedrooms have no windows, and there is a penetrating odor of sauerkraut. But the Germans do not care. They look forward to the time when they can afford a three-room apartment; and they would never willingly leave their beloved Kleindeutschland. The Americans who own all these buildings know this. That's why they do not consider improving the housing conditions. They like the Germans as tenants because they pay their rent, punctually, in advance, and keep the buildings neat and clean. The landlords are interested in keeping the German tenants crowded together because such buildings bring more profit than one-story houses. . . .

There are more inns in Kleindeutschland than in Germany. Every fourth house is an inn, and there is one for every 200 people. To the stranger, coming for the first time into the section, it would appear that there was nothing but beer saloons. Actually an immense quantity of beer is consumed. Since the German does not care for brandy there is not a single hard liquor saloon in Kleindeutschland. Wine is too expensive, so the resident has to be content with beer.

One who has not seen the Deutschländle on a Sunday, does not know it at all. What a contrast it presents to the American sections, where the shutters are closed, and the quiet of a cemetery prevails! On Sundays the . . . churches are full, but there is nevertheless general happiness and good cheer. The Protestant Germans do not indulge in much religious observance. They profess to be freethinkers, and do not go to church very often. On the other hand, the Catholic church on Third Street is always overcrowded. It was built from the voluntary contributions of the German workingmen. Saving the money out of their weekly pay, they have built the second largest, and the most beautiful, church in New York City. It has a big tower and three bells, and nearby is a school which the German children attend and where classes are conducted in German. . . .

Carl Schurz came to America from London where he had fled after the abortive German Revolution of 1848. He was destined to become the most honored of all German immigrants, and to play an historic part in the political and intellectual developments of the United States. This selection is a series of extracts from his Reminiscences, which cover some aspects of his career. (Source: Carl Schurz, The Reminiscences of Carl Schurz (New York, 1907.)

My young wife and myself sailed from Portsmouth in August 1852 and landed in the harbor of New York on a bright September morning. With the buoyant hopefulness of young hearts, we saluted the new world . . . .
After a visit to Congress I saw the decisive contest rapidly approaching, and I felt an irresistible impulse to prepare myself for usefulness, however modest, in the impending crisis and to that end I pursued with increasing assiduity my studies of political history and the social conditions of the Republic, and of the theory and practical workings of its institutions. To the same end I thought it necessary to see more of the country and to get a larger experience of the character of the people. Especially did I long to breathe the fresh air of that part of the Union, which I imagined to be the 'real America,' the great West, where new states were growing up and where I would have an opportunity for observing the formative process of new political committees working themselves out of the raw . . . .
Following his appointment as minister to Spain In the course of our conversation I opened my heart to Mr. Lincoln about my troubles of conscience. I told him that since recent events had made a warlike conflict with the seceding states certain, it was much against my feelings to go to Spain as Minister and to spend my days in the ease and luxury of a diplomatic position, while the young men of the North were exposing their lives in the field, in defense of the life of the Republic; that, having helped as a public speaker, to bring about the present condition of things, I thought I would rather bear my share of the consequences; . . .and that I should be glad to resign my mission to Spain and at once join the volunteer army. . . .
President Johnson obviously wished to suppress my testimony as to the condition of things in the South. after he had returned from his survey of the South I resolved not to let him do so. I had conscientiously endeavored to see Southern conditions as they were. I had not permitted any political considerations or any preconceived opinions on my part, to obscure my perception and discernment in the slightest degree. I had told the truth as I had learned it and understood it with the severest accuracy and I thought it due to the country that the truth should be known . . . .
I remember vividly the feeling which almost oppressed me as I first sat down in my chair in the Senate chamber. I had actually reached the most exalted public position to which my boldest dreams of ambition

had hardly dared to aspire.   I was still a young man, just forty.   Little more than sixteen years had elapsed since I had landed on these shores a homeless waif saved from the wreck of a revolutionary movement.   There I was enfolded in the generous hospitality of the American people opening to me, as freely as to its own children, the great opportunities of the new world.   And here I was now, a member of the highest law-making body of the greatest of republics.   Should I ever be able fully to pay my debt of gratitude to this country, and justify the honors that had been headed upon me? . . . I recorded a vow in my heart that I would at least honestly endeavor to fulfill that duty . . . that I would never be a sycophant of power nor a flatterer of multitude; that if need be, I would stand up alone for my conviction of truth and right; and that there could be no personal sacrifice too great for my devotion to the Republic.

GERMANS IN TEXAS-1854

Frederick Law Olmstead, touring the ante-bellum South as a special correspondent for the New York Times, came upon a German community in the vicinity of New Braunfels, as he traveled through south central Texas in 1854. His observations, recorded in a book he subsequently wrote, suggest the extent to which the Germans shaped the cultural patterns of the developing West.

(Source: Frederick L. Olmstead, A Journey Through Texas, or a Saddle-Trip on the Southwestern Frontier, New York, 1860.)

The first German settlers we saw, we knew at once. They lived in little log cabins, and had inclosures of ten acres of land about them. The cabins were very simple and cheap habitations, but there were many little conveniences about them, and a care to secure comfort in small ways evident, that was very agreeable to notice. So, also, the greater variety of the crops which had been grown upon their allotments, and the more clean and complete tillage they had received contrasted favorably with the patches of corn-stubble, overgrown with crab-grass, which are usually the only gardens to be seen adjoining the cabins of the poor whites and slaves . . . .

We were entering the valley of the Guadalupe river, . . . and had passed a small brown house with a turret and cross upon it, which we learned was a Lutheran church, when we were overtaken by a good-natured butcher, who lived in Neu-Braunfels, whence he had ridden out early in the morning to kill and dress the hogs of one of the large farmers . . . .

He had been in this country eight years. . . . The Germans, generally, were doing well, and were contented. They had had a hard time at first, but they were all doing well now---getting rich. He knew but one German who had bought a slave; they did not think well of slavery; they thought it better that all men should be free; besides, the negroes would not work so well as the Germans. They were improving their condition very rapidly, especially within the last two years . . . . There were Catholics and Protestants among them; as for himself, he was no friend to priests, whether Catholic or Protestant. He had had enough of them in Germany. They could not tell him anything new, and he never went to any church . . . .

We had still nearly a mile to ride before entering the town, and this distance met eight or ten large wagons, each drawn by three or four pairs of mules or five or six yokes of oxen, each carrying under its neck a brass bell. They were all driven by Germans, somewhat uncouthly but warmly and neatly dressed; all smoking and all good-humored, giving us "good morning" as we met. Noticing the strength of the wagons, I observed that they were made by Germans, probably.

"Yes," said the butcher, "the Germans make better wagons than the Americans; the Americans buy a great many of them. There are seven wagon-manufactories in Braunfels."

The main street of the town, which we soon entered upon, was very wide-three times as wide, in effect, as Broadway in New York. The houses, with which it was thickly lined on each side for a mile, were small, low cottages, of no pretensions to elegance, yet generally looking neat and comfortable. Many were furnished with verandahs and gardens, and the greater part were either stuccoed or painted. There were many workshops of mechanics and small stores, with signs oftener in English than in German; and bare-headed women, and men in caps and short jackets, with pendent pipes, were everywhere seen at work.

We had no acquaintance in the village, and no means of introduction, but, in hopes that we might better satisfy ourselves of the condition of the people, we agreed to stop at an inn and get dinner, instead of eating a cold snack in the saddle, without stopping at noon, as was our custom. "Here," said the butcher, "is my shop"---indicating a small house, at the door of which hung dressed meat and beef sausages---"and if you are going to stop, I will recommend you to my neighbor, there, Mr. Schmitz." It was a small cottage of a single story, having the roof extended so as to form a verandah, with a sign swinging before it, "Guadalupe Hotel, J. Schmitz."

I never in my life, except, perhaps, in awakening from a dream, met with such a sudden and complete transfer of associations. Instead of loose boarded or hewn log walls, with crevices stuffed with rags or daubed with mortar, which we have been accustomed to see during the last month, on staving in a door, where we have found any to open; instead, even, of four bare, cheerless sides of whitewashed plaster, which we have found twice or thrice only in a more aristocratic American residence, we were---in short, we were in Germany.

There was nothing wanting; there was nothing too much, for one of those delightful little inns which the pedestrian who has tramped through the Rhine land will ever remember gratefully. A long room, extending across the whole front of the cottage, the walls pink, with stenciled panels, and scroll ornaments in crimson, and with neatly-framed and glazed pretty lithographic prints hanging on all sides; a long, thick, dark oak table, with rounded ends, oak benches at its sides; chiseled oak chairs; a sofa, covered with cheap pink calico, with a small vine pattern; a stove in the corner; a little mahogany cupboard in another corner, with pitcher and glasses upon it; a smoky atmosphere; and finally, four thick-bearded men, from whom the smoke proceeds, who all bow and say "Good morning," as we lift our hats in the doorway.

The landlady enters; she does not readily understand us, and one of the smokers rises immediately to assist us. Dinner we shall have immediately, and she spreads the white cloth at an end of the table, before she leaves the room, and in two minutes' time, by which we have got off our coats and warmed our hands at the stove, we are asked to sit down. An excellent soup is set before us, and in succession there follow two courses of meat, neither of them pork and neither of them fried, two dishes of vegetables, salad, compote of peaches, coffee with milk, wheat bread from the loaf, and beautiful and sweet butter-not only such butter as I have never tasted south of the Potomac before, but such as I have been told a hundred

times it was impossible to make in southern climate.   What is the secret?
I suppose it is extreme cleanliness, beginning far back of where cleanliness usually begins at the South, and careful and thorough working.

We then spent an hour in conversation with the gentlemen who were in
the room.   They were all educated, cultivated, well-bred, respectful, kind,
and affable men.   All were natives of Germany, and had been living several years in Texas.   Some of them were travelers, their homes being in
other German settlements; some of them had resided long at Braunfels. . .

In the afternoon   of the following day   , we called upon the German
Protestant clergyman, who received us kindly, and, though speaking little
English, was very ready to give all the information he could about his
people, and the Germans in Texas generally.   We visited some of the
workshops, and called on a merchant to ascertain the quality and amount of
the cotton grown by the Germans in the neighborhood . . . .

As I was returning to the inn, about ten o'clock, I stopped for a few
moments at the gate of one of the little cottages, to listen to some of the
best singing I have heard for a long time, several parts being sustained
by very sweet and well-trained voices . . . .

In the morning we found that our horses had been bedded, for the
first time in Texas.

As we rode out of town, it was delightful to meet again troops of
children, with satchels and knapsacks of books, and little kettles of dinner,
all with ruddy, cheerful faces, the girls especially so, with their hair
braided neatly, and without caps or bonnets, smiling and saluting us---
"guten morgen"-as we met.

GERMAN LIFE IN AMERICA–1858

Karl Theodor Griesinger, a member of the "Forty-Eighter" contingent of Germans who came to America after the failure of the Revolution in Germany, wrote a succession of books on his travels in the United States and upon historical subjects. This selection is an extract from one of his works, which describes, with both humor and frustration, the life of Germans in America in the 1850's.
(Source: Karl Theodor Griesinger, Lebende Bilder Aus America (Stuttgart, 1858.)

A man who marries in Germany knows not his bride alone; he knows also her brothers and sisters, her parents and grandparents, her uncles and aunts, and her whole line of descent unto the third or fourth generation. He knows how the girl was brought up, the nature of her environment and relations, and the circumstances under which she lives. He knows the condition of her father; all the intricacies of inheritance and reversion are arranged in advance. The young pair can set forth on their life's journey with everything adjusted beforehand, children and deaths excepted.

How far different in America! The American is abrupt; he has no time to beat around the bush. He meets a girl in a shop, in the theater, at a ball, or in her parents' home. He needs a wife, thinks this one will do. He asks the question, she answers. The next day they are married and then proceed to inform the parents. The couple do not need to learn to know each other; that comes later.

The German in America is even worse off. Where in the world can he find a wife? He has little opportunity for family life. He generally lives in quarters that are too constricted to leave much room for the old amenities. And then, not a single day can be spared from his work without losing a critical day's wages. On Sundays though–well on Sunday, one must booze. So the young people get acquainted only in public places, in restaurants, concerts, the theater, balls. But what can they learn of each other there?---Everything, except that which relates to a wife and her duties.

And then, how many maidens are there in the United States born in the homeland or brought up after the German manner? Aren't they all long since Americanized, disdainful of newly arrived Germans, especially of the laborers?---But are there not enough newly immigrated girls? No question, but what kind of girls? Take a single trip on an immigrant ship, notice life as it's lived there, go below decks, where the travelers sleep in tiers by hundreds, think of the condition of the girls, how modestly and and bashfully they behave themselves within a single week, and how reserved they are after the second when they get to know the sailors! How could you think of marrying an imported bride! And even if she is "upright," do you know anything else about her or her family? How she looks, you see at once; how she views things only the future will tell.

In the last resort, you will be satisfied to drift into a marriage bureau and pay your half-dollar for a glimpse of the feminine daguerreotypes on display there. Or better still, you advertise in the papers. A hundred to one, you get a dozen answers. If you are willing to take one without a fortune, and don't demand a miracle of beauty, you will get at least two-dozen letters. Well now, read out the replies. There are people who claim to discern character from handwriting; but if you lack that ability, what do you do? You simply buy a pig in a poke; but remember, you can still take a look, and if she doesn't meet your requirements---the whole thing's off.

Or if you don't like this method, write to Germany, import a fresh blossom, and put your trust in the circumstance that she will come across with an "honest" family.

The main thing is, naturally, finding the bride; getting married is simplicity itself. There is no need for going to a minister unless you want to; civil officials will do as well. Any magistrate has power to perform the ceremony either in his office or in a restaurant. Every alderman can arrange a wedding. In a few minutes the whole thing is over. You pay your dollar and walk out with your wife. A wedding feast is also necessary unless perchance the minister who marries you is also an innkeeper (which often is the case) and sees to it that he gets the price of a few bottles of wine in addition to his fee.

There are no formalities, no hindrances, no questions as to age or status, no need of certificates of citizenship or residence. Your wife may be a Catholic, you a Jew, that is no obstacle. The permission of the church is as little necessary as that of the parents. As long as you are twenty-one and your bride at least fourteen then no one, nothing, can stand in your way, even were you her uncle, or she your aunt. It would be a fine thing if such "trifles" were questioned! Not more than a promise is necessary in America to marry. Many reckon it superfluous even to go through the procedure of a ceremony, and simply live together. Their children are legitimate, for open cohabitation between man and wife in the eyes of the law is worth as much as a knot tied in a church. The rights of women are well protected in the United States! . . . .

No matter how unfortunate may be the marriage of Germans in America, it shines by comparison with the marriage of a German and an Irishwoman. Language, in truth, is a barrier easily overcome---but, Irish and German habits . . . Ten times out of eleven she is drunk when you come home, and if you deprive her of money and warn the grocer to grocer to give home, and if you deprive her of money and warn the grocer to give her no credit, whe will simply pawn one piece of furniture, one garment after another, to be able to buy whiskey. And what will she cook for you! Sauerkraut and Bratwurst? Your very obedient servant-tough beefsteak or stewed fish. The food is ready in five minutes, and you cannot persuade her to work for you for more than five minutes. Say something to her, and she scolds back; notice how quick she is with her tongue and how prompt in reference to the damned Dutchmen. In dealing with an Irishwoman only blows are understood.

And in the final extremity marry an American girl, then, poor German, you are really lost; in her eyes you always remain a despised German. So it goes for the Germans who marry in America. Nothing but ease!

The grocer is always a German countryman. Before these people came to New York the Americans must have run these businesses themselves. But for a long time it has been quite different; these Germans have a monopoly of groceries. And there are few such Germans who in their lifetime have not been grocers, or, at least, expected to be.

Who has not seen a grocery cannot possibly imagine what is contained therein. The grocer carries everything except krametsvögel and church steeples. There will be found: sugar and coffee, tea and chocolate, cheese and eggs, milk and bread, hams and sausages, brushes and brooms, snuff and cigars, kindling wood and soap, cords and firewood, charcoal and coal, radishes and sauerkraut, beets and cucumbers, beans and lentils, whiskey and wine, beer and cider, oil and vinegar, pepper and salt, shoe polish and onions, starch and toothpowder, butter and washtubs, fats and smoked bloaters, dried apples and turnips, rice and sliced pears, plums and juniper berries, herrings and salted meats, onion cookies and leeks, potatoes and horseradish, honey and Cologne pipes, polishing powder and bricks for the cook stove, mustard and writing paper, candles and thread, needles and dyes, and hundreds of other articles. On his platform are brought together stockings, shoes, cloths, linens-in short anything that a man, who does not wish to live like a Hottentot, might need in his household.

A grocery is, wherever possible, located on a corner, and, in the more thickly settled districts of the cities, there are always four groceries on the corners where two streets cross. A corner shop is visible from all sides and he is no fool who chooses such a place.

The grocer is no fool. True, he was only a poor bumpkin at home, watching the swine, chasing the geese. He lived off rye bread and smoked bacon, dressed in ragged castoffs and in a twenty-year-old leather jacket. He went to school as little as possible, having no time for it, and learned enough reading and writing to be able to scrawl his signature and to spell out the words in the Bible. He grew up wild, without culture, knowledge, or understanding, not even by hearsay. But one thing he did learn, an essential for America, how to reckon. And even that he learned not in school, but at home. His mother was accustomed during her pregnancy to repeat a long multiplication table instead of paternosters, and so stamped it into him from the start. He had only to fall back on this memory to master the whole art of counting without teachers of method.

He understood also one thing more, worth as much as his facility in reckoning-to do without.

When the high German comes to New York, his first call is for good food and drink. He must make up for the long sea voyage. The south German soaks himself in wine and lager, the north German in whiskey and beer. But the low German drinks nothing. He drags the last morsel of bacon rind from his pocket and gnaws upon it until the pangs of hunger pass. Then he is on his way to seek out his uncle, cousin, godfather, whomever he knows who has written him to come and sent the passage money, that is, just enough to get him across the cheapest class of the cheapest boat, on the cheapest Liverpool route. Naturally, this relative has a grocery, and the newcomer is well received, gets a tumbler-full of whiskey and a great slab of bacon. After a half-hour he is at home and is shown what he has to do . . . .

The low German strips off the marks of foreignness in a short time. After a single year he is no longer green, and no one can discern how short a time he has been in the country. In that respect he profits from his occupation and his language. To the shop of his cousin or uncle come all sorts of people, men of all nations, south Germans, north Germans, Jews, Irish, Americans, English. The grocer serves all alike, that is, he takes from all their money, and that the young newcomer learns right quickly. Presbyterian or Methodist, Catholic or Protestant, Unitarian or Mormon, Atheist or Jew, it is all one to him. Their money is one thing. And then, he learns the language so quickly. Not that he has any particular linguistic talents, not that any scraps of Latin or French he may have picked up earlier are of any use, but low German is already half English, they sound alike and many words are identical. A good pecentage of English words are derived from the low German. And then, there is the daily contact with English-speaking people, which serves the young German even better than the young Jew.

After two years the young peasant lad has become a proper clerk; that is, he speaks English well and understands the business from top to bottom. His pay has climbed from four to eight dollars a month, and it is now time to look for a better position. His relative actually helps him look about and he ends up in the place of another German where things operate on a larger scale. The cousin, uncle, or godfather does not lose thereby, for he simply imports another lad who starts at four dollars a month.

fter four years it occurs to the clerk to set up in business for himself. He has saved up a hundred or two hundred dollars and found a friend who has as much again. One fine Sunday, the two are off to see the grocer with whom they served their apprenticeship. The grocer notices what is up at once. The back room, behind the shop, is opened and a flask of good old brandy loosens tongues. The two have learned that the grocer has opened a new enterprise or that he contemplates investing in a wholesale house, and they have come to purchase his store. Naturally the few hundred dollars are not enough; but the relative will give them credit for the rest, and with the last glass the bargain is sealed. On Monday the new bosses move in, the old moves out. After a few years they have paid off their debts, and in a few more each partner owns his own store.

Such is the way of the world, at least for the low Germans.

The German's greatest vexation is the Sunday law. He must keep his shop closed on that day, but likes to earn his money every day. Nevertheless, he knows how to help himself; every store has its back door, well known to the customers when the front door is closed.

The grocer's greatest joy comes from the sale of liquor. He buys by the gallon at thirty or thirty-six cents and sells by the glass for three, by the half-pint for six cents, a mere matter of 150 to 300 per cent profit. Whether the whiskey is whiskey, or well cut, is still another matter.

A few people are unkind enough to charge that there is something peculiar about his weight and that his gallon measure is a half-pint too short. It may be that here and there a few minor errors creep in. Who is to blame if the scale, with the passage of time, gets off balance, or if the tinsmith puts too little tin into the measures?

Three peculiar characteristics mark off the low German grocer from all other Germans: he cannot tolerate lager, he does not sport a mustache, and he cannot believe that people will not lie when they have the opportunity.

So much for the grocer! . . . .

But then, what else could the Americans do on the sacred Sunday? Boredom alone would bring them there! "Six days shalt thou labor and on the seventh shalt thou rest." Reasonable men have understood this to mean that Sunday should be a day for the relaxation of body and soul. The Americans have arranged matters, however, so that the rest of Sunday is the rest of the tomb. And they have enacted laws that make this arrangement compulsory for all.

On Sunday no train moves, except for the most essential official business; no omnibus is in service, no steamer when it possibly can help it. All business places are closed, and restaurants may not open under threat of severe penalties. A gravelike quiet must prevail, says the law, and you may buy neither bread, nor milk, nor cigars, without violating the law. Theaters, bowling alleys, pleasant excursions---God keep you from even dreaming of such things! Be grateful that you are allowed in winter to build a fire and cook a warm supper.

People who make such laws must be half crazy; these Sunday laws are mad enough! Travel in any New England city, in Rhode Island, Massachusetts or Connecticut, in Pennsylvania and New Jersey, indeed anywhere except in New York, Cincinnati, and Saint Louis, everywhere you will find pleasure places closed, restaurants, theaters, shops shut tight, all means of communication halted, all the streets empty, the whole city a cemetery. And what about the country? The farmer rides ten miles to his church, then ten miles home, and sleeps. That is his rece
then ten miles home, and sleeps. That is his recreation. A wonderful discovery, the Sunday law! A very peculiar way indeed to serve the Lord! It certainly must amuse the angels above to observe the self-scourging down below.

The pious American sits in his parlor, rocks in his easy chair, his feet spread out before him, and smokes cigar after cigar. Now and then he summons up energy to get to the cabinet and take a good swig out of the brandy bottle; by evening he has put away enough to forget the passage of time. And his wife? She sits across from her husband and also rocks, holding her prayer book upside down, nods her head as if in sleep, and in the evening is overjoyed when a friend of the family appears. And the These rush also to church in the morning, but particularly are fond of the evening prayer meetings and of walking home with an escort.

This is an American Sunday. On no other day, at no other hour, does the German feel more deeply that he is a stranger in a strange land, and always will remain a foreigner.

The Irishman-well, he is satisfied with his whiskey bottle. He gets it filled on Saturday and, if necessary, can replenish his stock at the apothecary who is, naturally, not closed on Sunday, and who carries rum and brandy, only at a slightly higher price.

But the German, with his love of music and song, with his joy in God's free nature, with his inclination toward companionship and Gemütlichkeit, with all his recollections of a Sunday in the old homeland, what has he got? Dear reader, I'll tell you what he has---lonely homesickness. Only one recourse is open to him. He tiptoes across, taps on the back door of a familiar saloon and, if he is known as loyal, not an informer, then the tightly shut door opens to reveal his friends sitting in the gaslight, with the windows tightly sealed so that no ray of light can reach the street, making a good night of it in the middle of the day, and drinking beer besides. "Six days shalt thou labor in the sweat of thy brow, and on the seventh shalt thou drink lager to thine heart's content, but secretly and by theft, like a thief in the night." Thus do the Germans interpret the Sunday law. They've no alternative.

Of course, nothing of this appears in the letters home that persuade other people to come across. There is not a hint that your Sunday's recreation is "stealthily and secretly, mutely, deep in silence, without songs or the clink of glasses, without sunshine or promenade, to drink your high-priced beer."

The Germans have actually often tried to transfer their Sundays to Mondays, but to do so they would have to work on Sunday, and that is not allowed by their masters. It sometimes reaches a point where one goes on a spree Monday morning to get in what is out of reach on Sunday.

But New York is quite different. If the Americans have discovered the Sunday law, the New York Germans have discovered the "Sacred Concert"; God bless the discovery. At the "Sacred Concert" pure church music is performed. The Sunday papers carry long announcements of such concerts in German restaurants. Even the German theater presents a sacred concert. If you go to the theater you will find that the sacred music never gets to be presented. In fact it will seem to you that a comedy is being offered, with perhaps some pleasant music between the acts. And in the restaurants it will sound as if there were Strauss waltzes issuing forth from the trumpets. It may be a little difficult to recognize the church music in the billiard games, the target practice with air guns, the amusing performance of the yodelers, the gymnastic leaps of an acrobat, even the tinkling sounds of the beer glasses. The whole place is thick with people, men and women all sit with full glasses before them, munch on bread and cheese, and do their souls good. This sacred music is certainly worth its twelve-cent admission fee.

Let the American saints grumble over this German Sunday; let them send for the police because the place is open. New York is a cosmopolitan city and will not fall into the hands of the preachers. In any case, the words "Sacred Concert" are enough; church music is allowed on Sundays. . . .

The selection describes the horrible conditions aboard the ships bringing German immigrants to the United States during the late 1860's. It also shows that even passengers who paid their own way were helpless at the hands of the ship owners and captains. (Source: Friedrich Kapp, Immigration and the Commissioners of Immigration (New York, 1870.)

The Leibnitz, originally the Van Couver, is a large and fine vessel, built at Boston for the China trade, and formerly plying between that port and China. She sold some years ago to the house of Robert M. Sloman, and has since sailed under her present name.

We were informed that her last trip was her second with emigrants on board. Last summer, she went to Quebec with about seven hundred passengers, of whom she lost only a few on her passage; this time, she left Hamburg, November 2, 1867, Capt. H. F. Bornhold, lay at Cuxhaven, on account of head-winds, until the 11th, whereupon she took the southern course to New York. She went by the way of Madeira, down to the Tropics, 20th degree, and arrived in the Lower Bay on January 11, 1868, after a passage of 61 days, or rather 70 days-at least, as far as the passengers are concerned, who were confined to the densely crowded steerage for that length of time.

The heat, for the period that they were in the lower latitudes, very often reached 24 degrees of Reaumur, or 94 degrees of Fahrenheit. Her passengers 544 in all--of whom 395 were adults, 103 children, and 46 infants---came principally from Mecklenburg, and proposed to settle as farmers and laborers in Illinois and Wisconsin; besides them, there were about 40 Prussians from Pomerania and Posen, and a few Saxons and Thuringians . . . .

Of these 544 German passengers, 105 died on the voyage, and three in port, making in all 108 deaths---leaving 436 surviving.

The first death occurred on November 25th. On some days, as for instance on December 1, nine passengers died, and on December 17, eight. The sickness did not abate until toward the end of December, and no new cases happened when the ship had again reached the northern latitudes. Five children were born. During the voyage some families had died out entirely; of others, the fathers or mothers are gone; here, a husband had left a poor widow, with small children; and there, a husband had lost his wife. We spoke to some little boys and girls, who, when asked where were their parents, pointed to the ocean with sobs and tears, and cried, "Down there!"

Prior to our arrival on board, the ship had been cleansed and fumigated several times, but not sufficiently so to remove the dirt, which, in some places, covered the walls. Mr. Frederick Kassner, our able and experienced Boarding Officer, reports that he found the ship and the passengers in a most filthy condition, and that when boarding the Leibnitz he hardly discovered a clean spot on the ladder, or on the ropes, where he

could put his hands and feet. He does not remember to have seen anything like it within the last five years . . . .

As to the interior of the vessel, the upper steerage is high and wide.
All the spars, beams, and planks which were used for the construction of
temporary berths had been removed. Except through two hatchways and two
very small ventilators, it had no ventilation, and not a single window or
bull's-eye was open during the voyage. In general, however, it was not
worse than the average of the steerages of other emigrant ships; but the
lower steerage, the so-called orlop-deck, is a perfect pesthole, calculated
to kill the healthiest man. It had been made a temporary room for the
voyage by laying a tier of planks over the lower beams of the vessel, and
they were so supported that they shook when walking on them. The little
light this orlop-deck received came through one of the hatchways of the
upper-deck. Although the latter was open when we were on board, and although the ship was lying in the open sea, free from all sides, it was impossible to see anything at a distance of two or three feet. On our enquir-
ing how this hole had been lighted during the voyage, we were told that some
lanterns had been up there, but on account of the foulness of the air, they
could scarcely burn. It had, of course, much less than the upper-deck
draft or ventilation, and was immediately over the keel, where the bilge-
water collects, and adjoining part of the cargo, which consisted of wool and
hides. And in this place about 120 passengers were crowded for 70 days,
and for a greater part of the voyage in a tropical heat, with scanty rations
and a very inadequate supply of water, and worse than all, suffering from
the miasma below, above, and beside them, which of itself must create
fever and pestilence!

The captain himself stated to us that the passengers refused to carry
the excrements on the deck, and that "the urine and ordure of the upper-
steerage flowed down to the lower." As the main-deck was very difficult
of access from the orlop-deck, the inmates of the latter often failed to go
on deck even to attend to the calls of nature. There were only six water-
closets for the accommodation of all the passengers. They have been
cleansed, of course; but the smell that emanated from them was still very
intense, and corroborates the statement of the above-named officers-that
they must have been in an extraordinary frightful condition.

When the ship Lord Brougham, belonging to the same line, arrived
on the 6th of December last, from Hamburg, and had lost 75 out of 383
passengers, we personally examined the majority of the survivors, and
found them not only healthy and in good spirits, but, at the same time, in
every respect satisfied with the treatment they had received on board.

The present case, however, is different. There was not a single
emigrant who did not complain of the captain, as well as of the short allowance of provisions and water on board. As we know, from a long experience, that the passengers of emigrant ships, with a very few exceptions,
are in the habit of claiming more than they are entitled to, we are far
from putting implicit faith in all their statements. There is as much
falsehood and exaggeration among this class of people as among any
other body of uneducated men. We have, therefore, taken their complaints
with due allowance, and report only so much thereof as we believe to be
well founded.

All the passengers concur in the complaint that their provisions were short, partly rotten, and that, especially, the supply of water was insufficient, until they were approaching port. We examined the provisions on board, and found that the water was clear and pure. If the whole supply during the voyage was such as the samples handed to us, there was no reason to complain as to quality. But, in quantity, the complaint of the passengers are too well founded; for they unanimously state, and are not effectually contradicted by the captain, that they never received more than half a pint of drinkable water per day, while by the laws of the United States they were entitled to receive three quarts. Some of the biscuit handed to us were rotten and old, and hardly eatable; other pieces were better. We ordered the steward to open a cask of corned-beef and found it of ordinary good quality. The butter, however, was rancid. Once a week herrings were cooked instead of meat. The beans and sauerkraut were often badly cooked, and, in spite of hunger, thrown overboard.

The treatment of the passengers was heartless in the extreme. The sick passengers received the same food with the healthy, and high prices were exacted for all extras and comforts. A regular traffic in wine, beer, and liquors was carried on between the passengers on the one side and the steward and crew on the other . . . .

When the first deaths occurred, the corpses were often suffered to remain in the steerage for full twenty-four hours. In some cases the bodies were covered with vermin before they were removed.

There was no physician on board. Although we found a large medicine-chest, it was not large enough for the many cases of sickness, and was, in fact, emptied after the first two weeks of the voyage.

The captain seems to have been sadly deficient in energy and authority in matters of moment, while he punished severely small offences; as, for instance, he handcuffed a passenger for the use of insulting words; but he did not enforce the plainest rules for the health and welfare of his passenger for the use of insulting words; but he did not enforce the plainest rules for the health and welfare of his passengers. Instead of compelling them, from the first, to come on deck and remove the dirt, he allowed them to remain below, and to perish among their own excrements. Of the whole crew, the cook alone fell sick and died, as he slept in the steerage. Three passenger girls who were employed in the kitchen, and lived on deck, enjoyed excellent health, during the whole voyage.

The physicians . . . to whose report we refer for particulars, most positively declare that it was not the Asiatic cholera, but intestinal and stomach catarrh . . . more or less severe, and contagious typhus, which killed the passengers. From what we saw and learned from the passengers, we likewise arrive at the conclusion that the shocking mortality on board the <u>Leibnitz</u> arose from want of good ventilation, cleanliness, suitable medical care, sufficient water, and wholesome food.

The intensity of feeling by Americans against German-Americans
during the first World War was almost over-powering. German-
Americans felt this hostility in many ways. This selection, written by a German-American, describes some aspects of this xenophobia.
(Source: Julius Drachsler, Democracy and Assimilation: The
Blending of Immigrant Heritages in America (New York, 1920.)

The declaration of war by Congress seemed to have silenced all
dissenting voices. Henceforth there was only one goal for all loyal Americans, a complete and crushing victory over the arrogant German war-ma-
chine. Among the immigrants, the psychological characteristics of the pre-
war period were brought into still stronger relief. Organization of "loyalty leagues" grew apace. Passage of resolutions of "unflinching loyalty
to our country, the United States of America" became part of the regular
order of business of every immigrant social organization. Spontaneous
requests were made by Czecho-Slovaks, Poles, Jews, Armenians, to the
government to organize foreign legions as distinct fighting units in the
American army, while the international composition of the American expeditionary forces was pointed out as proof of the unanimity of spirit among
the native and the foreign born. Relief campaigns for sufferers in the war
zones were inaugurated on a scale unimaginable before the War.

Nor were patriotic societies, and the government slow to take advantage of the rising tide of feeling among the foreign-born and to harness this
dynamic sentiment to urgent national tasks that had to be carried through
as pre-conditions of final victory.

Simultaneously with these positive efforts to awaken and stiffen the
will to fight to the bitter end, there developed a definite anti-German propaganda throughout the country. The slow, but relentless coercion of a
changing public opinion manifested itself in all degrees of suppression.
Sensitive citizens, bearing unmistakable "American" names. Local communities rechristened streets and avenues, business concerns and social welfare agencies appealed to their clients and patrons in the name of the "new
management." But these self-imposed metamorphoses were, after all,
only superficial and mild in their effects. Much more stringent were the
attempts to have Federal and State authorities revoke the charters of incorporated German-American societies; to have municipalities prohibit
the sale of German papers by barring them from news-stands; to persuade
advertisers not to use the German language press; to prevail upon news-
dealers not to sell these publications; to hold mass-meetings to stir up
sentiment in favor of a press in the English language only. This hostile
attitude towards the German language and German culture was clearly
reflected in the action of the State and local school authorities of almost
forty States of the Union. German was either banished from the curricula
of many public schools and high schools by direct order of the educational
authorities, or by the refusal of students to elect it as a language study

where they had the option to do so. The effort was made to stimulate interest in other languages as substitutes, such as Spanish and French. Text books, magazines or newspaper publications were sedulously censored or excluded from the schools, lest they might serve as channels of insidious German propaganda. In one city the German texts were not only taken from the students but "tons of the volumes were burned as though they were under the ban." Another community "not only put the German text books out of the schools but provided cans in the principal streets, where pupils and the public might throw all the volumes they wished to have destroyed."

As the war-fever rose, serious doubts began to be expressed by many earnest citizens as to the sanity of the German people in permitting the awful carnage to go on at such a fearful cost to themselves. An enterprising student of national psychology even suggested in a letter to the editor of a metropolitan daily, the appointment of a scientific commission to study the "German type of mind."

THE GERMAN-AMERICAN BUND-1939

With the rise of Adolf Hitler in Germany in the 1930's, the principal transmitter of the Nazi doctrine in the United States was the German-American Bund, organized in 1936. The most sensational display of Nazi influence came on the night of February 20, 1939, when 22,000 members of the Bund held a rally at New York's Madison Square Garden. This selection is a description of that rally as reported in the local press.

(Source: New York Times, February 21, 1939.)

Protected by more than 1,700 policemen, who made of Madison Square Garden a fortress almost impregnable to anti-Nazis, the German-American Bund last night staged its much-advertised "Americanism" rally and celebration of George Washington's Birthday.

The meeting itself was orderly enough, the only out-of-the-way incident inside the Garden occurring near the end when a young Jewish listener mounted the platform, only to be tackled by several uniformed Bund members and then carried off by a half-dozen husky policemen. Mention of President Roosevelt and other critics of Nazi Germany drew resounding boos.

Outside, in the several blocks immediately adjacent to the big sports arena, there was scattered fighting and disorder before, during and after the meeting, but no serious trouble . . . .

There the meeting started off peacefully, distinguishable from any other George Washington Birthday celebration only by the anti-Jewish, pro-Nazi banners, the uniformed Bund members and the Bund emblems and flags, with the singing of "The Star-Spangled Banner," by Miss Margarete Rittershaus.

There were cheers as James Wheeler-Hill, national secretary of the Bund, opened the meeting with the salutation, "My fellow Christian Americans," and introduced the Rev. S. G. Von Bosse, Lutheran minister of Philadelphia, who pleaded for a renunciation of all "isms," including Nazism.

The cheers turned to jeers and boos, however, as other speakers mentioned President Roosevelt---made to sound as though it were spelled "Rosenfeld"---Harry Hopkins and others who have been outspoken in their denunciation of Nazi Germany. Cheers, however, greeted the names of former President Herbert C. Hoover and Senators Gerald P. Nye, Hiram Johnson and William E. Borah.

G. W. Kunze, national public relations director of the Bund, was the speaker to mention the President's name.

He said the country was in a deplorable state "When Henry Morgenthau takes the place of an Alexander Hamilton and Franklin D. Roosevelt the place of a Washington."

It was announced that a collection would be taken up and the 3,000 uniformed Bund members, called Ordnungsdienst men, began passing through the audience, whose members had paid from 40 cents to $1.10 for their tickets. The amount that was collected was not immediately announced.

It was an enthusiastic audience that gave close attention to every speaker, and roared a mass response when called on to pledge allegiance to the flag. The word "undivided allegiance to the Flag."

Fritz Kuhn, national Fuehrer of the Bund movement since 1935 and one of Hitler's original followers in Munich in 1923, as the chief speaker of the rally, declared that he and his followers were determined "to protect themselves, their children and their homes against those who would turn the United States into a bolshevik paradise."

He denounced the "campaign of hate" he said was being waged against the organization in the press, the radio and the cinema "through the hands of the Jews."

"We do not say all Jews are Communists," he continued.

"We do not say all Jews are Communists," he continued, "but we do say that the Jew is the driving force of communism."

From there he went on to read the roll of Jewish leaders whom he blamed for many of America's troubles past and present, mentioning among others Haym Solomon, the Jewish financier of the Revolutionary War, Bernard M. Baruch and Samuel Untermyer.

As Mr. Kuhn neared the end of his speech a young man in a blue suit made a single-handed attempt to steale the platform. A dozen grey-shirted Bund members grabbed him as he reached the rostrum and threw him to the floor. Several policemen immediately took charge and carried him struggling through an opening directly behind the stage. His trousers were torn off in the process . . . .

Only thirteen arrests were made, all on minor charges. Eight persons received medical aid because of minor injuries, four of them policemen. Another policeman was knocked down by a police horse, but declined aid. A Bund member inside the Garden was treated at Polyclinic Hospital for scratches on his head.

Potentially the most serious situation arose when the Bund followers began to stream out the doors when the meeting closed at 11:15. As they passed through the police lines at Fifty-second Street some of the more violent anti-Nazis in the crowd began assaults on individuals. Policemen quickly broke up those fights and by 12 o'clock Eighth Avenue was as quiet as it usually is at that hour on a midweek midnight.

There was considerable delay in vehicular traffic along the avenue from 6 P.M. to 12, traffic being diverted entirely for a few minutes at 11:15, and the whole area for two blocks north, south and east of the Garden was closed off for the same period to foot pedestrians not bound for the rally.

BIBLIOGRAPHY

The bibliography that follows barely scratches the surface of the vast amount of various books and articles that have been written about German immigration in the United States. And, yet, despite this voluminous amount of material, the Germans have been written about imperfectly, despite their great numbers, their numerous institutions, and their many communities in America. However, there are many works of great value concerned with the subject, and some of them are cited in this bibliography.

My aim is to suggest useful further reading to people who do not regard themselves as specialists in this field, or to those who wish to pursue the study of the German-Americans still further. Several of the titles listed are in German, for no bibliography about German-Americans and German immigration would be respectable without a sampling of books and articles about this topic written in the German language, of which there are several hundred. In addition, only a few German language newspapers have been cited, since a complete listing of these papers would require much more space than this bibliography has been allotted.

Despite these shortcomings, this bibliography provides an excellent starting point for the interested student who can then investigate for himself additional, and, or contradictory materials. Comments have been made on certain selected books which the author deemed most useful. Unfortunately, there is no single respository of all the materials concerned with German-Americans, and the various works are scattered in libraries and collections throughout the United States.

Adler, Jacob. Claus Speckels; The Sugar King of Hawaii. Honolulu, 1967.

American-German Review. Philadelphia. Carl Schurz Memorial Foundation. This series of review issues contain much valuable information about very specific topics in the history of the Germans in the United States.

Baker, Thomas S. Lenau and Young Germany in America. New York, 1897.

Bancroft, Frederick, ed. Speeches, Correspondence, and Political Papers of Carl Schurz. New York, 1913. This is perhaps the best and most complete single volume on the works of Carl Schurz. Contains most of his important public documents.

Barnard, Harry. The Eagle Forgotten; The Life of John Peter Altgeld. Indianapolis, 1938. An excellent, full biography of the German-American Mayor of Chicago.

Barry, Colman J. The Catholic Church and the German-Americans. New York, 1953. Contains some interesting insights into the struggle between the German and Irish Catholics for power in the United States.

Bek, Whitfield J. "Benjamin Franklin and the German Charity Schools," Proceedings of the American Philosophical Society. XCIX, 1955.

Benjamin, G. G. Germans in Texas. New York, 1910. Contains much valuable information on the German migrations to Texas, but is rather outdated in some ways. This whole area needs reexamining.

Bercovici, Konrad. "German Settlers in the United States." Century, CX, October, 1925.

Bess, F. B. Eine Populaere Geschichte der Stadt Peoria. Peoria, 1906.

Bienhoff, Esther. "Diary of Heinrich Egge, A German Immigrant." Mississippi Valley Historical Review. XVII, 1930-1931. An excellent primary source for the journey and settlement of one German immigrant, but in many respects, typical of thousands of others.

Biesele, Rudolph L. The History of the German Settlements in Texas, 1831-1864. Austin, Texas, 1930. Most of the book deals with the German settlement at New Braunfels.

Birnheim, G. D. History of the German Settlements and of the Lutheran Church in North and South Carolina. Philadelphia, 1872.

Bittinger, Lucy, The Germans in Colonial Times, New York, 1906. One of the classic works on the subject. Another area that needs new work.

Blum, Virgil C. "The Political and Military Activities of the German Element in St. Louis, 1859-1861." Missouri Historical Review, XLII, 1947-1948.

Braxton, F. "German Colonial Patriots." National Republic. XIX, April 1932. A series of short biographical sketches of a number of German Revolutionary War heroes.

Bruncken, Ernest. "The Political Activity of the Wisconsin Germans, 1854-1860." Proceedings of the State Historical Society of Wisconsin. 1901.

Buffington, Albert F. A Grammatical and Linguistic Study of Pennsylvania German. Harvard Ph.D. Thesis, 1936. A fascinating breakdown of the vernacular language spoken in the Pennsylvania Dutch regions.

Child, Clifton J. "German-American Attempts to Prevent the Exportation of Munitions of War, 1914-1915." Mississippi Valley Historical Review. XXV, December, 1938.

------------------. The German-Americans in Politics, 1914-1917. New York, 1939. Probably the most valuable work on this subject up to the present time.

Connelley, W. E. Heckewelder's Narrative and Journal, 1797. Cleveland, Ohio, 1907.

Cunz, Dieter. The Maryland Germans. Princeton, New Jersey, 1948. A Massive compilation of material, examining practically every aspect of the subject.

David, Henry. The History of the Haymarket Affair. New York, 1936. Deals with this important incident in a thoroughly scholarly way.

Davis-Dubois, Rachel, and Schweppe, Emma. The Germans in American Life. New York, 1936. A popular, very laudatory study of German contributions to American society and culture.

Deutsche Pionier, der Cincinnati, 1869-1887. An extremely important German language newspaper. Excellent source for German-American History. Its attitude was largely "New German."

Diffenderfer, F. R. The German Immigration into Pennsylvania Through the Port of Philadelphia, 1700-1775. Lancaster, Pennsylvania, 1900.

Dorpalen, Andreas. "The German Element and the Issues of the Civil War." Mississippi Valley Historical Review. XXIX, 1942.

------------------"The German Element in Early Pennsylvania Politics, 1789-1800.'' Pennsylvania History. IX, 1942. An excellent article showing the tremendous influence and voting strength possessed by the Germans of Pennsylvania during these years.

------------------"The Political Influence of the German Element in Colonial America." Pennsylvania History. VI, 1939.

Duden, Gottfried. "Bericht Über eine Reise nache den Westlichen Staaten Nordamerikas." Published in installments in Missouri Historical Review. XII, XIII, 1917-1919. This is one of the best contemporary accounts of America in the early eighteenth century by an immigrant who traveled around the United States and recorded his observations.

Easum, Chester V. The Americanization of Carl Schurz. Chicago, 1929. A classic study on the life and times of the great German-American.

Eiboeck, Joseph. Die Deutschen von Iowa und derren Errungensch aften. New York, 1924.

Emery, Charles W. "The Iowa Germans in the Election of 1860." Annals of Iowa. XXII, 1940.

Evers, Fritz. Zion in Baltimore. Baltimore, 1930. Interesting study of German Moravian settlement and activity in and around Baltimore, Maryland.

Faust, Albert B. The German Element in the United States. 2 vols. Boston, 1929. This is still the most outstanding work in the field, covering the topic from a variety of vantage points.

------------------."What Germany has Given America." Our World. III, April, 1923. Highly laudatory in its praise of German contributions to the culture and society of the United States.

Feer, Robert A. "Official Use of the German Language in Pennsylvania." Pennsylvania Magazine of History and Biography. LXXVI, 1952.

Fiske, Jon. The Dutch and Quaker Colonies. 2 vols. Boston, 1899. An old, but still useful work on early German settlement in colonial America,

Florer, W. W., ed. Liberty Writings of Dr. Hermann Kiefer. New York, 1917.

Fogel, Edwin M. Beliefs and Superstitions of the Pennsylvania Germans. Philadelphia, 1915. An extremely interesting book for those interested in the life style of the Pennsylvania Dutch.

Francke, Kuno. Cotton Mather and August Hermann Francke. Boston, 1896.

------------------"German Characters and the German-Americans." Atlantic Monthly. CXXXVII, April, 1926.

------------------German Ideals of Today. New York, 1907. Contains a good deal of valuable material on the character and philosophy of the German-American, although rather dated.

Fries, Adelaide L. Records of the Moravians in North Carolina. 7 vols. Raleigh, North Carolina, 1922-1947. This set of works is a massive collection of statistics, documents, biographies and memorabilia of the settlement, growth and developement of the Moravian Germans in North Carolina. Very complete in so far as it goes.

------------------The Moravians in Georgia, 1735-1740. Raleigh, North Carolina, 1905. Dated, but about the best in its field of study.

Froebel, Julius. Aus Amerika. Erfahrungen, Reisen, und Studien. 2 vols. Leipzig, 1858. This work acted as a kind of guidebook and propaganda agent for prospective German immigrants.

Fuess, Claude. Carl Schurz, Reformer, 1829-1906. New York, 1932. An excellent biography, colorfully written and well documented.

Gehring, K. "German-American As A Citizen." Open Court. XL, January, 1926.

Gehrke, William H. "The Transition from the German to the English Language in North Carolina." North Carolina Historical Review. XII, 1935.

Glanz, Rudolf. Jews in Relation to the Cultural Milieu of Germans in America up to the 1880's. New York, 1947. Highly sophisticated work concerned with the phychology and attitudes of the German Jews, and their place within German-American culture and society.

------------------"German-American Political Thought." Deutsch-Amerikanische Geschichtsblaetter. XXC, 1925.

Goebel, Julius. Das Deutschthum in den Vereinigten Staaten von Nord Amerika. Munich, 1914. An excellent, but biased study of Germans in the United States written by the long time editor of the very influential German-American Historical Society Review, Deutsch Amerikanische Geschichtsblaetter.

Goepp, Charles, and Poesche, Frederick. The New Rome. New York, 1852. Rather old work describing the evolving German-American culture in Missouri settlements, ie. Hermann. Very pro-German.

Goldmark, Joseph. Pilgrims of '48. New Haven, Connecticut, 1930. Fair version of the story of the migration to the United States by the political refugees of the abortive German Revolution of 1848.

Gongaware, George J. The History of the German Friendly Society of Charleston, South Carolina, 1776-1916. Richmond, Virginia, 1935.

Graffenried, Christopher von. Account of the Founding of New Bern. Raleigh, North Carolina, 1920. Deals with the founding of a Palatine German colony in North Carolina in 1710. Written by the leader of the immigrants and translated from the original German in 1920.

Hagedorn, Herman. The Hyphenated Family, New York, 1960. An interesting work detailing life and problems of German-American families.

Hall, Norman S. The Balloon Buster: Frank Luke of Arizona. New York, 1928. Stirring biography of the famous German-American air ace of World War I.

Hansen, Marcus L. "The Revolutions of 1848 and the German emigration." Journal of Economic and Business History. II, 1930. Deals with the movement of the Forty Eighters to America, but places some emphasis on their economic motives for emigrating.

Hark, Ann. Hex Marks the Spot. Philadelphia, 1938. Popular account of the customs and traditions of the Amish people of Lancaster County, Pennsylvania.

Harlow, Albin F. The Serene Cincinnatians, New York, 1950. Interesting account of the leading German-American families of Cincinnati in the development and growth of that city.

Hawgood, John A. The Tragedy of German-America. New York, 1940. A detailed description of a German minority attempting to replant the ways of old Germany in the New World in nineteenth century Missouri.

Hense-Jensen, Wilhelm. Wisconsin Deutsch-Amerikaner. 2 vols. Milwaukee, 1909. Old, but quite valuable study of Wisconsin German-Americans from their beginnings in that state to about 1900.

Herriot, F. I. "The Conference of the German-Republicans in the Deutsches Haus, May 14-15, 1860." Illinois State Historical Society Journal. 1928. Discusses the German-American strategy to be used at the Republican National Nominating Convention in 1860.

------------------"The Germans in the Gubernatorial campaign of Iowa in 1859." Deutsch-Amerikanische Geschichtsblaetter. XIV, 1914.

------------------"The Germans of Chicago and Stephen A. Douglas." Deutsch-Amerikanische Geschichtsblaetter. XII, 1912.

Hillard, George S. Life and Letters and Journal of George Ticknor. Boston, 1876. Excellent primary source for examining the influence of German educational techniques on American schools and colleges.

Hillquit, Morris. History of Socialism in the United States. New York, 1903. A fine book as far as it goes, dealing with the development of Socialism in the United States, with particular emphasis on the role played by the German-Americans in its growth and philosophy.

Hirshler, Eric F., ed. Jews From Germany in the United States. New York, 1955. Recent study of the German Jews, their attitudes and contributions to American society.

Hocker, Wilhelm. Germantown, 1683-1933. Philadelphia, 1933. Good study of the founding and growth of the first large Mennonite colony in the United States.

Holden, Vincent F. The Yankee Paul: Issac Thomas Hecker. Milwaukee, 1958. Interesting work on the life of a German Lutheran who made the rare conversion to Catholicism, spent time at Brook Farm, and was a forerunner of the ecumenical-liberal humanist movement.

Holmes, Fred L. Old World Wisconsin. Eau Claire, Wisconsin, 1944. General study on the development of the state of Wisconsin. Contains valuable information on the German settlements.

Horne, A. R. Horne's Pennsylvania German Dialect. Baltimore, 1889. Dated, but amusing "dictionary" of the vernacular used in Pennsylvania Dutch country.

Huhn, Heinrich. "Gedenkblatt." Amerikanischer Turner-Kalender. 1886-1887. Two articles consisting of biographical sketches of members of the Turnerbund.

Ismas, Felix, Weber and Fields. New York, 1924. Interesting, humorous biography of the great comedy team of vaudeville days.

Jacobs, H. E. A History of the Evangelical Lutheran Church in the United States. New York, 1893. Highly laudatory work on the origins, growth and development of this distinctly German religious organization.

Johnson, H. B. "The Election of 1860 and the Germans in Minnesota." Minnesota History, XXVIII, March, 1947.

------------------"The German Forty-Eighters in Davenport." Iowa Journal of History and Politics. XLIV, January, 1946.

Johnson, William T. "Some Aspects of the Relations of the Government and German Settlers in Colonial Pennsylvania, 1683-1754." Pennsylvania History. XI, 1910. Old but valuable article on a complex aspect of German settlement in Pennsylvania.

Joll, James. The Anarchists. Boston, 1964. Highly provocative study of the German-American anarchists involved in the Haymarket Affair in Chicago. Up to date version of the incident.

Jordan, Terry G. German Seed in Texas Soil: Immigrant Farmers in the Nineteenth Century. Austin, Texas, 1966. Scholarly, fresh account of the German settlements in Texas, especially New Braunfels. Well written, and documented, with some interesting new insights.

Kamman, William F. Socialism in German-American Literature. Philadelphia, 1917. This aspect of the German-American experience needs some new work. This study, however, presents some interesting interpretations through the words of some of the leading German Socialists.

Kapp, Friedrich. Immigration and the Commissioners of Emigration of the State of New York. New York, 1870. A classic work in the field of immigration history, written by a German immigrant who was appointed a member of the Commissioners of Emigration. Contains many primary documents and statistics.

Kerstein, Edward S. Milwaukee's All-American Mayor: A Portrait of Daniel Webster Hoan. New York, 1966. Excellent biography of the six term Mayor of Milwaukee, who provided an inspiration for the German Socialists of that city.

Knittle, W. A. Early Eighteenth Century Palatine Emigration. New York, 1936. Traces the movement of Palatine Germans first to New York and later to Pennsylvania and Maryland. Very detailed work.

Koerner, Gustav. Memoirs of Gustav Koerner, 1809-1896, Life Sketches Written at the Suggestion of His Children. 2 vols. Cedar Rapids, Iowa, 1909. One of the best contemporary accounts of German-American life, written by an early nineteenth century immigrant who was one of the leaders of the intellectuals in the German community.

Kolodin, Irving. "The German Influence on the Metropolitan Opera." The American-German Review. March, 1936.

Koss, Rudolf A. Milwaukee. Milwaukee, 1871. Old, but still valuable work on this city as far as it goes. Attitude and approach basically German.

Kuhns, Oscar. German and Swiss Settlements in Pennsylvania. New York, 1901. Detailed treatment of the various settlements in Pennsylvania, with special emphasis on the Mennonites.

Lacher, J. H. A. The German Element in Wisconsin. Milwaukee, 1925. A Good study, but concentrates too much on the rural German-Americans.

Learned, M. D. The Life of Franz Daniel Pastorius. Philadelphia, 1908. The only biography of this important Mennonite leader, who led his followers to Pennsylvania in 1683.

------------------The Pennsylvania German Dialect. Baltimore, 1889.

Lemke, Theodore. Geschichtedes Deutschums von. New York von 1848 bis 1892. New York, 1891-92. Traces the story of the German Forty-Eighters who settled in New York. New work on this topic needed.

Lenel, Edith. Friedrich Kapp, 1824-1884. Liepzig, 1935. An excellent biography on this important German-American leader and intellectual.

Leucks, F. A. H. Early German Theater in New York, 1840-1872. New York, 1928. Fascinating study of the growth of this art form among the Germans in New York City.

Levering, Joseph M. A History of Bethlehem, Pennsylvania, 1741-1892. Bethlehem, Pennsylvania, 1903. The definitive work on the first major German-Moravian settlement in the United States. Laden with important information.

Mansfield, J. B. The History of Tuscarawas County, Ohio. Chicago, 1884. While dated, this work on the Separatist Society of Zoar still contains much valuable data.

Meng, John J. "Cahenslyism: - The First Stage, 1883-1891" Catholic Historical Review. XXXI, 1945-1946. Excellent article dealing with the late nineteenth century struggle for power in the Catholic Church between the German and Irish-Americans.

------------------"Cahenslyism: The Second Chapter, 1891-1910." Catholic Historical Review. XXXII, 1946-1947. Continuation of the above article detailing the consequences and results of this struggle.

Metzner, Henry. A Brief History of the American Turnerbund. Pittsburgh, 1924, As the title indicated, this book is too short a study to do justice to such an important German-American movement.

Meyer, Ernest L. Bucket Boy: A Milwaukee Legend. New York, 1947. Interesting social study of German life in Milwaukee by the son of a German-American newspaper editor.

------------------"Twilight of a Golden Age." American Mercury. XXIX, August, 1933. Colorful article depicting the last glorious years of German society in Milwaukee.

Meyer, T. P. "The Germans of Pennsylvania: Their Coming and Conflicts With the Irish." Pennsylvania German. VIII, 1907.

Meynen, Emil. Bibliography on German Settlements in Colonial North America. Leipzig, 1937. Invaluable work detailing all of the studies on German colonial settlements up to 1937.

Mittleberger, Gottlieb. Journey to Pennsylvania. Philadelphia, 1898. Excellent account of the Atlantic crossing by a German immigrant who came in 1750.

Monaghan, Jay. "Did Abraham Lincoln Receive the Illinois German Vote?" Illinois State Historical Review. XLVII, 1941. A provocative article presenting new light on a crucial aspect of the 1860 election.

Muench, Friedrich. Gesammelte Schriften. St. Louis, 1902.

Nau, John F. The German People of New Orleans, 1850-1900. Leiden, 1958. Modern, scholarly book on the settlement of Germans in the South. Deals with community life and leadership among the German element in that city.

Nead, D. W. The Pennsylvania-German Settlement of Maryland. Lancaster, Pennsylvania, 1914. Old, but useful work concerned with eighteenth century movement of Mennonites and Palatines into Maryland.

O'Connor, Richard. Black Jack Pershing. New York, 1961. Colorful, stirring biography of America's great military hero of World War I. Well written.

------------------The German-Americans: An Informal History. Boston, 1968. Newest work on the German-Americans to date. Good biography and dramatic narrative, but lacks adequate documentation. Nevertheless a satisfying book.

Ohlinger, Gustavus. Their True Faith and Allegiance. New York, 1917. Attempts to dispell charges of disloyalty among German-Americans during World War I.

Olmsted, Frederic L. A Journey Through Texas; or A Saddle Trip on the Southwestern Frontier. New York, 1859. While dealing with Texas in general, this work contains valuable information on the early German settlements there.

Palmer, John M. General Von Steuben. Port Washington, New York, 1937. Very good biography of the colonial German General who fought in the American Revolution.

Pershing, E. J. The Pershing Family in America. Philadelphia, 1926. Detailed geneology of the Pershing family written by a member of that family from 1749 to 1925.

Porter, Kenneth W. John Jacob Astor, Business-Man. Cambridge, Massachusetts, 1931. Excellent biography of the famed millionaire although old.

Ratterman, H. A., ed. Deutsch-Amerikanisches Magazin. Cincinnati, 1887. An excellent source for German-American history.

------------------. Gustav Körner. Chicago, 1903. A detailed and very laudatory biography of the great German-American intellectual and pioneer of the nineteenth century.

Rauschning, Herman. The Voice of Destruction. New York, 1940. A contemporary view of the Nazi influence among German-Americans in the 1930's.

Reeves, A. M. The Founding of Wineland the Good. London, 1890.

Reid, W. M. The Mohawk Valley; Its Legends and History. New York, 1908. General study of this upper New York State region with especial emphasis on the Germans who settled and lived there.

Remak, Joachim. "Friends of the New Germany: The Bund and German-American Relations." Journal of Modern History. XXIX, 1957. Excellent article concerned with the growth of the German-American Bund and its affects on American relations with Nazi Germany.

Riedesel, Baroness Friederike. Letters and Journals Relating to the War of the American Revolution. Chapel Hill, North Carolina, 1965. Revealing contemporary source of the American Revolution by a German noblewoman.

Rogge, O. John. The Official German Report: Nazi Penetration, 1924-1942. New York, 1962. An excellent study of the German-American Bund by perhaps the best expert on the subject.

Rombauer, Robert J. The Union Cause in St. Louis in 1861. St. Louis, 1909. Good book describing German role in keeping Missouri in the Union.

Rosengarten, Joseph. The German Soldier in the Wars of the United States. Philadelphia, 1886. Old and highly laudatory study of German-American military participation. Several good short biographies included.

Rothan, Emmet H. The German-Catholic Immigrant in the United States, 1830-1860. New York, 1946. Very scholarly, well written and well documented study of the coming, settlement and growth of the German Catholic element in the United States.

Russell, John A. The Germanic Influence in the Making of Michigan. Detroit, 1927. Detailed work, but rather overdone as far as German influence in Michigan is concerned.

Schaefer, Joseph. Intimate Letters of Carl Schurz. Madison, Wisconsin, 1928. Valuable collection of some lesser-known correspondence of the German-American statesman.

Schinnerer, Paul O. "Karl Heinzen, Reformer, Poet and Literary Critic." Deutsch-Amerikanische Geschicktsblaetter. XV, 1915.

Schlegel, C. W. German-American Families. New York, 1917. Series of short biographical and geneological sketches of important German-American families in the United States up to 1917.

Schneider, Carl E. The German Church on the American Frontier. St. Louis, 1939. Deals with the religious activities of the Lutherans in the settlement of the mid-west.

Schrader, Frederick F. The Germans in the Making of America. New York, 1924. Fair general history of the German experience in the United States.

Schrott, Lambert. Pioneer German Catholics in the American Colonies. New York, 1933.

Schuricht, Hermann. History of the German Element in Virginia. Baltimore, 1898. Old but valuable study of German settlement. Contains important information of that area.

Schuyler, Hamilton. The Roeblings; A Century of Engineers, Bridge-builders and Industrialists. Princeton, New Jersey, 1931. Very good biography of the Roebling family with major emphasis on John and Washington Roebling.

Schurz, Carl. Reminiscences. New York, 1917. Contains a wealth of information on the German element as well as general American history of the nineteenth century.

Seabrook, William. These Foreigners. New York, 1938. General history of immigrant groups with some good material on the Germans.

Shuster, George N. The Forty-Eighter in America. Washington, D. C., 1948. Traces the German Forty-Eighter emigration to the United States and discusses their work and contributions to American life.

Smith, B. "Feast in the East." American Magazine. CXXI, April, 1936.

Smith, C. H. Mennonite Immigration to Pennsylvania. Philadelphia, 1929.

Smith, Henry C. The Story of the Mennonites. Berne, Indiana, 1941. Popular history of this German Religious group.

Society for the History of Germans in Maryland, Reports. Baltimore, 1887. Invaluable for work on early German settlement in Maryland.

Spaeth, Sigmund. Fifty Years with Music. New York, 1959. Contains a mass of information on the German-American contribution to music in the United States.

Staats-Zeitung, New Yorker. Excellent newspaper source for New York City history, as well as for German-American history.

Stevens, Walter Barlow. St. Louis, The Fourth City, 1764-1911. St. Louis, 1911. Good biography of the city as far as it goes with some fine chapters on the Germans.

Still, Bayrd. Milwaukee: The History of a City. Madison, Wisconsin, 1948. The best volume written on Milwaukee. Very detailed with excellent bibliography.

Stroebel, P. A. The Salzburgers and their Descendents. Baltimore, 1855. Dated, but still contains worthwhile information on an aspect of German immigration, that needs some new investigation.

Tappert, Theodore G. "Henry Melchior Mühlenberg and the Revolution." Church History. IX, 1942. An interesting article on the patriot-pastor of the American Revolution and the Lutheran Church.

Thuring, Charles F. The American and the German University. New York, 1928. Important book for understanding influence of German educational system on American colleges.

Townsend, Andrew J. "The Germans of Chicago." Deutsch-Amerikanische Geschichtsblaetter. XXXII, 1932.

Wakin, Edward, and Scheuer, Joseph F. The De-Romanization of the American Catholic Church. New York, 1966. A very important book on the development of a national Catholic Church in the United States, and the part German Catholics played in this movement.

Walker, Mack. Germany and the Emigration, 1816-1885. Cambridge, Massachusetts, 1964. Deals with the various problems in Germany that motivated emigration to the United States.

Wallace, Paul A. Conrad Weiser, 1696-1766. Philadelphia, 1945. Solid biography on the famous German furtrapper, Indian fighter, pioneer of early colonial days.

Ward, Gertrude. "John Ettwein and the Moravians in the Revolution." Pennsylvania History. I, 1934.

Wayland, James W. The German Element of the Shenandoah Valley of Virginia. Charlottesville, Virginia, 1908.

Weaver, Glen. "Benjamin Franklin and the Pennsylvania Germans." William and Mary Quarterly. XIV, 1957. An excellent article on a little-known aspect of Franklin's life.

------------------"The Lutheran Church During the French and Indian War." Lutheran Quarterly. VI, 1954. Very scholarly article with excellent primary sources.

Weber, S. E. "The Germans and the Charity School Movement." Pennsylvania German. VIII, 1907. An old, but still valuable piece of work.

Weygandt, Cornelius. The Red Mills: A Record of Days Outdoors and In with Things Pennsylvania Dutch. Philadelphia, 1929. One of the best books on the subject. Very colorful and interesting.

Wittke, Carl. German-Americans and the World War. New York, 1936. One of the best works written on this very tragic chapter of German-American history.

------------------. "German Contributions to America." World Tomorrow. XII, March, 1929.

------------------. "Marx and Weitling." Essays in Political Theory. Ithaca, New York, 1948. Brilliant essay on the two great communist theoreticians.

------------------. Refugees of Revolution; The German Forty-Eighters in America. New York, 1952. Excellent study of these political refugees and their part in the growth of the United States.

------------------. We Who Built America. Englewood Cliffs, New Jersey, 1939. One of the best books of the history of American immigration. Several great chapters on the German element.

------------------. The German-Language Press in America. Louisville, Kentucky, 1957. Scholarly study on the German press.

------------------. "Wilhelm Weitling's Literary Efforts." Monatschefte. XL, 1948.

------------------. Against the Current. Chicago, 1944.

Wood, Ralph, ed. The Pennsylvania Germans. Princeton, New Jersey, 1942. Contains very valuable information on all aspects of life among the Pennsylvania Germans. Written by several authors who are experts in the various areas.

Zimmerman, G. A. Deutsch in Amerika. Chicago, 1892.

Zucker, A. E., ed. The Forty Eighters. New York, 1950. Very detailed and complete history of this important political group of German refugees. Contains about fifty short biographical sketches of the leading Forty-Eighters.